Coils, Folds, Twists, and Turns

CONTEMPORARY TECHNIQUES IN FIBER

TRACY JAMAR

STACKPOLE BOOKS

Guilford, Connecticut

Published by Stackpole Books
An imprint of Globe Pequot
www.rowman.com

Distributed by NATIONAL BOOK NETWORK
800-462-6420

British Library Cataloguing in Publication Information Available

Library of Congress Cataloging-in-Publication Data is available.

ISBN 978-0-8117-1658-1 (paperback)
ISBN 978-0-8117-6538-1 (ebook)

Printed in the United States of America

♾™ The paper used in this publication meets the minimum requirements of American National Standard for Information Sciences—Permanence of Paper for Printed Library Materials, ANSI/NISO Z39.48-1992.

To all who appreciate, encourage, and pursue
the making of things by hand—past, present, and future.

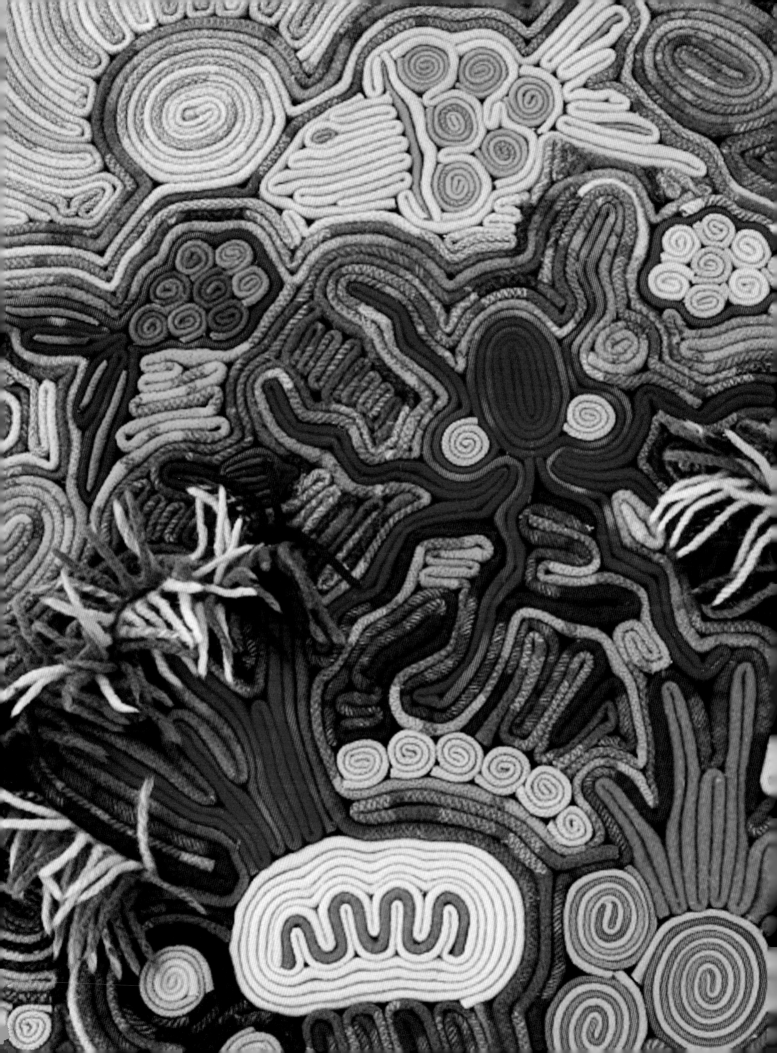

Contents

Introduction

My attraction to handmade antique textiles and associated accoutrements has been active since childhood. I made a thirty-plus-year career restoring and conserving antique hooked rugs and quilts; first at America Hurrah Gallery and then on my own as Jamar Textile Restoration Studio, both in New York City.

In 2009, I completed a college degree studying American history through women's handmade textiles at Goddard College in Vermont. One area of particular interest was American handmade rugs; interwoven with that was a growing interest in contemporary fiber art. Balancing my love of antique textiles, especially early sewn rug-making techniques that predated rug hooking, I started creating my own fiber works incorporating and combining many of the techniques I had become familiar with while restoring antique textiles.

Through the years I became friends with other people who shared my interests. One of these was Jan Whitlock, a dealer specializing in early and exquisite antique textiles, who had just started to write a book on early handmade rug forms and wondered if I would be interested in participating. The book, *American Sewn Rugs: Their History with Exceptional Examples* by Jan Whitlock with Tracy Jamar, published in 2012, explores a genre of rugs made primarily in the first half of the nineteenth century. Through changes in industrialization, societal manners, and manufacturing of textiles, the making of hooked rugs supplanted those earlier methods in mid-century.

Those early techniques, some being various forms of shirring, intrigued me—why had they gone out of fashion and use? While making rug samples for the book using these early techniques, at least one of the reasons became very clear: They took a lot of time and materials compared to rug hooking. Nevertheless, I thought the techniques gave lovely and exciting results, and I started using them in my contemporary fiber work. Later, I became aware of other forms, called standing wool and coiling, that had commonalities with the earlier techniques. There seemed to be spontaneous and random eruptions of these techniques being incorporated into the rug hooking/contemporary fiber art world.

After giving a workshop on shirring during Rug Hooking Week at Sauder Village in Ohio in August 2013, I was offered the opportunity to write about those techniques. This book is about the fabric manipulation techniques of shirring, standing wool, and coiling and their variations.

If you are already familiar with them, I hope you will discover new ways to incorporate them in your work. If you are new to these techniques, I hope you will be entranced enough to try them in your work. I will explain how to create and use these various forms and how they can be combined with other techniques to expand your repertoire of fabric manipulations to add interest and texture to your rugs, hangings, personal accessories, and fiber art.

Some of the terms and ideas may be familiar or new. Some have a history that is traceable to a point in antique rug making, as already mentioned, while others have a history not as clearly defined, having developed in a less-documented manner. All have become incorporated in contemporary fiber work much more recently. This is not so much about the history of where these techniques originated, but an introduction and encouragement as to how you may use them to create, embellish, and enhance your fiber work.

These techniques can be used singly or in combination with other techniques to expand your handwork repertoire. Only basic sewing skills and tools are needed, and most any kind of fabric can be worked. In the Patterns and Projects chapters, I have combined various fabrics and techniques to show you the variety of results that are possible and how they look when worked, as well as to suggest other options with the hopes that you will explore possibilities beyond what is shown here.

The Gallery chapter gives a glimpse at how other fiber artists have explored and engaged with these techniques in myriad ways. Finally, I have included a resource listing that, although far from comprehensive, will lead you to other sites and sources of interest.

I encourage you to experiment and discover what is possible, letting unexpected results—formerly known as mistakes—lead you to effects and outcomes that enhance your work. Let these techniques intrigue you, pique your interest, and inspire you to explore and play with them in your own fiber work.

When defining the various categories, terms, and techniques, there are bound to be overlaps and inconsistencies. Factor in the variances in regional terms and definitions, and it can seem a bit confusing, if not contradictory. I have done my best to maintain constancy throughout; if and when I do not use the terms with which you are most familiar, please accept my apologies.

Whether these techniques and ideas are new or familiar to you, I hope you find the comfort and satisfaction that comes to those who do handwork. The materials, designs, colors, and uses change with each decade and generation—what does not change is the pleasure of the work, the camaraderie with others, and a connection to previous and future makers. We all become part of the historical continuum that documents our time through handwork and textiles. Play, discover, and have fun!

CHAPTER 1

Antique Rug History and Techniques

In the early nineteenth century, many handmade rugs were created with a variety of techniques—several shirring variations as well as yarn-sewn, patched, and appliquéd rugs are from that period. These early handmade rugs were regarded as showpieces of handwork, not just utilitarian household objects. Making these rugs required skill, time, and material; at least two of those were not available to any but the wealthiest.

Though not nearly as well documented as samplers of the same era have been, some of these early rug-making techniques were taught at schools for girls from well-to-do families. Originating as an upper-class enterprise, these rug-making forms became nearly obsolete after the mid-nineteenth century. At that time more and more manufactured goods became available to a rising middle class. Styles changed and women across the economic spectrum were able to buy more of that which they once had to make themselves.

Technological improvements in all forms of manufacturing—especially textile production—allowed fabrics to be made more inexpensively. That, along with the greater availability of burlap, allowed women from lower economic levels to find rug hooking to be a perfect form to express themselves and provide an inexpensive way to decorate their homes. Rug hooking was also, not inconsequentially, markedly quicker to do when compared to the various forms of shirring.

As this nineteenth-century Canadian rhyme suggests, rug hooking became associated with old, worn, reused clothing and a "make do, waste not" attitude.

I am the family wardrobe, best and worst
Of all our generations, from the first:
Grandpa's Sunday-go-to-meetin' coat,
and the woolen muffler he wore at his throat;
Grandma's shawl, that came from Fayal;
Ma's wedding gown,
Three times turned and once let down,
Which once was plum but now turned brown;
Pa's red flannels that made him itch;
Pants and shirts;
Petticoats and skirts;
From one to the other, but I can't tell which.
Tread carefully,
Because, you see,
If you scuff on me;
You scratch the bark of the family tree.

Urn with Flowers, *antique chenille-shirred wool and yarn on linen, 30" x 42" (76.2 cm x 106.7 cm), circa 1850. Private collection of Mrs. Stephenson.*

TRACY JAMAR

Blue Basket of Flowers, *antique bias-shirred and yarn-sewn wool on linen, 33" x 56" (83.8 cm x 142.2 cm), circa 1800–1830. Private collection of Jan Whitlock.*

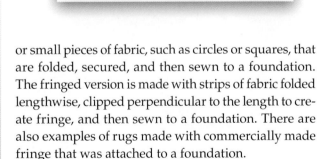

Although the economic and societal changes of the time augured the near loss of those earlier rug-making forms and heralded the rise of rug hooking, the shirred techniques offer some of the most interesting and textural effects that can be incorporated into contemporary hooked pieces and other fiber art.

Shirring

Shirring refers to techniques used in the making of hand-sewn rugs, most created between 1820 and 1850. These rugs were made from material that was fashioned and manipulated in a number of ways and then sewn to a foundation. There are several variations of shirring: bias, chenille, bundled, fringed, and pleated. The first two are made with narrow strips of fabric that are gathered (slightly with bias, more fully with chenille) and sewn to a foundation.

One of the other variations is one Jan Whitlock and I labeled "bundled" in our book *American Sewn Rugs: Their History with Exceptional Examples*. These rugs were made using short, narrow strips of fabric or short lengths of yarn that are tied up in little bundles and/

or small pieces of fabric, such as circles or squares, that are folded, secured, and then sewn to a foundation. The fringed version is made with strips of fabric folded lengthwise, clipped perpendicular to the length to create fringe, and then sewn to a foundation. There are also examples of rugs made with commercially made fringe that was attached to a foundation.

These forms of construction were dependent on a thread securing the decorative elements to a fairly sturdy foundation, which meant they were not as durable to heavy use as a woven or pile rug would be. We ascertained that they were more commonly used for decorative purposes or in areas of minimal use.

TRACY JAMAR

Fine Feathered Flowers, *antique bias-shirred silk on linen, 33.5" x 23" (85.1 cm x 58.4 cm), circa 1820–1840. Private collection of Tracy Jamar and Monty Silver.*

Nested Triangles, *antique bias-shirred wool on linen with replaced binding, 17" x 29" (43.2 cm x 73.7 cm), circa 1830–1840. Private collection of Tracy Jamar.*

Standing Wool

Whereas wealthier households were more likely to have shirred rug examples, standing wool seems to have been popularized by folks of more modest means. The makers used worn-out clothing or fabric leftovers to create allover patterns for their rugs and mats. How far back the form goes would be hard to ascertain, as it is likely that these rugs, a variant of rag rugs, were used in a more utilitarian manner than the fancier shirred examples, and therefore fewer of them have survived.

Standing wool uses strips of fabric that are manipulated in folds, coils, and gathers and then sewn to each other. These strips can be used singly, in multiple layers sewn as one, or made extra wide and folded in half lengthwise (used with the fold up or down) before assembling and stitching them in a symmetrical radiating pattern or free-form design. As they are sewn with flat sides together, the edges of the strips become the visible surface of the rug.

As its name would suggest, standing wool is substantial enough to be its own support; often made without a foundation, it is therefore reversible. The name seems to be a contemporary descriptive term, and though the technique has been used for a long time, it too is gaining in popularity as a "new" technique.

Rugs can be made exclusively with the standing wool technique, but the form and its variations are being used more and more in conjunction with other techniques. The strips, single or folded, can be coiled as part of the design, used in undulating lines or switchback sections, wrapped around other elements, or worked as a single length or with another strip of a different color for interesting design purposes.

Historically, standing wool rugs and mats were sewn; today, some prefer to use glue (preferably glue formulated for fabrics). Many standing wool pieces today use thick fabric such as blanket- and coat-weight wools, but lighter weights can also be effective. It is also a method that allows a mat or rug to be used and be a work in progress simultaneously—just add another row and the piece is larger.

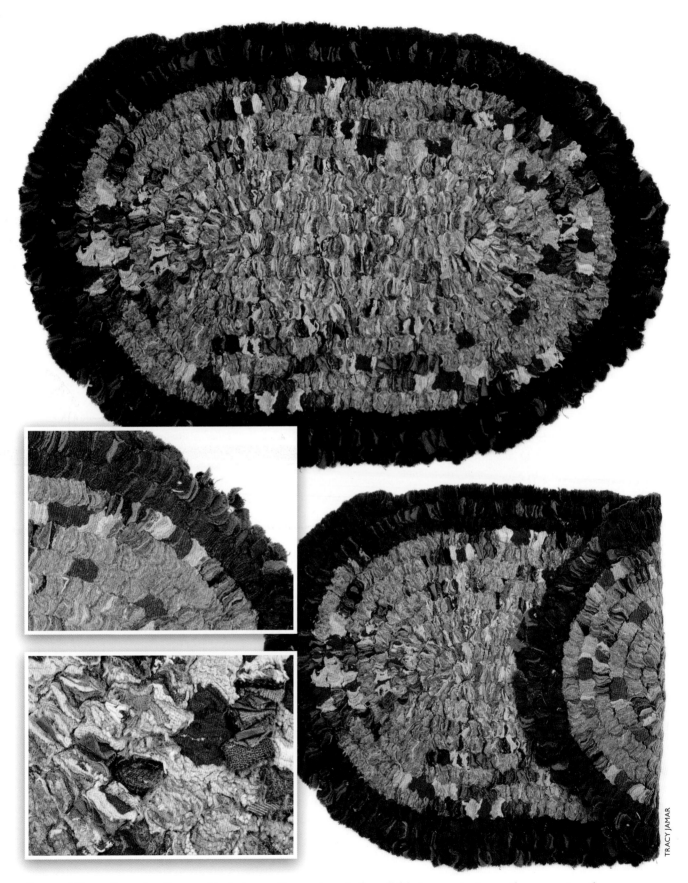

Square Bits, *antique standing wool technique with assortment of small fabric squares strung then sewn together, 17.5" x 26.5" (44.5 cm x 67.3 cm), circa 1900. Private collection of Tracy Jamar.*

TRACY JAMAR

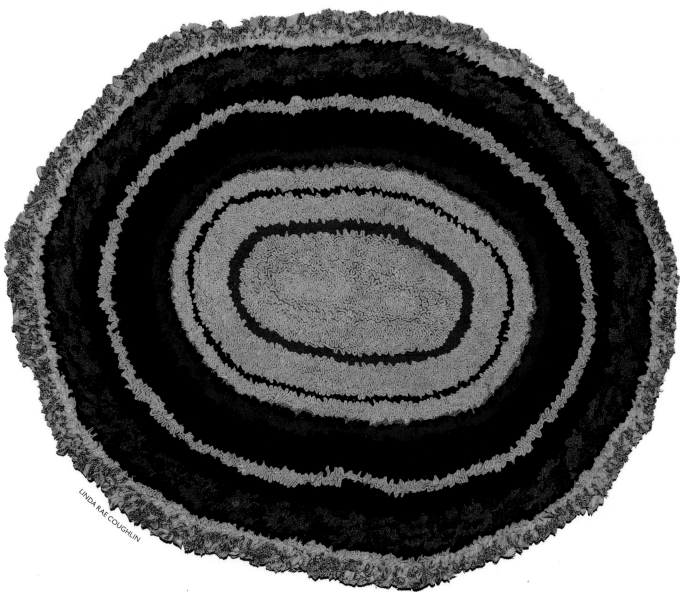

Oval Rug with Rings, *antique shirred standing wool,*
26" x 31" (66 cm x 78.7 cm), circa 1925. Private collection of Linda Rae and Jerry Coughlin.

There are several areas where one might be confused as to whether something qualifies as standing wool versus chenille shirring. I consider gathered strips of thicker wool that are then sewn to each other as the sole means of support to be standing wool. Make the fabric lighter weight and sew it to a foundation, and I am more likely to call it chenille shirring. Mix in a couple of variables, and it can be a tail chase trying to define absolute terms for each. Confusion is not my intent; I hope to show how discovering these marvelous ways to manipulate fabric will set you on an adventure. Do not let the definitions, delineations, and crossover of terms get in the way of exploring new techniques.

Coiling

Coiling is a form of standing wool, but since it has its own distinct form, it garners a classification of its own. This process, which produces small rolls of fabric and is known by a number of names—coiling, quilling, standing wool circles, beading, scrolling, spooling, and possibly others—is a simple technique with delightful results.

The origin of the process is unknown, and it is likely one of those things that just happens, as one can find the same patterning in hoses, belts, cookies, pastries, ropes, snakes, clock springs, ribbons, scrollwork, and hairstyles—it is a handy way to neatly store long thin objects. Who has not taken a strip of fabric from their hooking or braiding project and wrapped it into a coil? When those coiled strips of fabric are gathered together, a delightful arrangement can be fashioned. It has become more widely used in the last decade, not just as an embellishment, but as a technique for entire works.

It is not a leap to see the connection to the paper craft art form of quilling, hence one of the popular names for this technique. Scrolling is the term the artists Steven and William Ladd (http://www.stevenandwilliam.com) used in their artwork consisting of coiled lengths of cotton belt webbing (acquired from a factory going out of business) and exhibited at the Parrish Art Museum in Southampton, New York (http://parrishart.org/exhibitions/steven-and-william-ladd-mary-queen-universe).

Beading, a term coined by Diana Blake Gray, is easy to understand; the small coils do resemble beads, and assembling them in a line or on a string or thread is very much like beading.

For the sake of continuity in this book I will refer to those rolled-up strips of fabric as *coils* and the process of making them as *coiling*. They are either sewn to each other in self-support or to a foundation. If the coils are only attached to each other, the assemblage could be reversible and it would likely be referred to as *standing wool*. As you will see, there is a lot of crossover and blending of techniques.

CHAPTER 2

Getting Started

The variety of effects from these techniques will enhance any piece of fiber handwork; they look wonderful used individually or combined with other methods. The more one experiments and explores these techniques, the more ways one thinks of how they can be implemented.

There is no one way or even best way to make the elements; it depends on the fabric, the effect you want to achieve, how your work will be used, and your particular sewing skills and preferences. As these forms are held together with thread and stitches (and in some cases, glue), they may not withstand active floor use, as can other rug-making forms. Their durability depends on several considerations: the fabric used, the techniques, and how the elements are used, such as whether they are flush with the surrounding surface or if embellishments rise above the surface.

These instructions explain how I make the elements. Some of them may seem a bit involved; I am a process person and find the journey as interesting as the destination. This is intended to get you started. I hope that these instructions will lead you to discover a manner of working that is exciting and satisfying.

Supplies

This list is a general inventory of the supplies you will need to create fiber art using the techniques in this book. You will not need all of the items on the list for every project.

Foundation—sturdy fabric or hooking foundation

Fabrics—various weights of wool, silk, cotton, synthetics, and blends; possibly ribbons and yarns

Needles—long, stout, curved, beading

Pins—regular and/or long, with colored heads

Pliers and/or needle grabber

Thread—regular and heavy duty

Stretcher frame or hooking frame

Stapler and staples

Scissors (straight and/or pinking), rotary cutter and board, or strip cutter

Tailor's chalk/pencil/markers

Tissue and pattern-making paper

Pattern/design

Measuring tape or ruler

Fusible webbing or fusible interfacing

Thimbles, if you use them

FABRIC

How often has it happened that you see a fabric you love, but when hooked or otherwise manipulated it has a totally different look than you expected? Fabric will look very different coiled or shirred than it does flat or hooked. Look at the edges (crosswise, lengthwise, and bias), even roll a bit of the edge to see how it reads. The edge is what will be seen in most of these techniques; see if it has a look and color you like.

It is not only color, but quality, thickness, fiber content, and the type of weave that will give various results. Whether fabric is cut on the bias or straight of the grain or torn adds yet more variables. Thicker wools are good for either cutting or tearing, will have a bulkier shape, and are likely to have better durability than looser weaves. Looser or lighter weaves are easier for folding or gathering in narrower strips. They may unravel more easily, though, so it may be better to cut on the bias rather than tear them; however, a raveled look may be desirable for certain effects.

I encourage you to try a variety of fabrics from challis thin to coat-weight thick. Even strips cut from old sweaters will give interesting results. In the samples and patterns for this book I have used wool, silk, cotton, and fabrics of unknown blends, each offering something different. Likely you will settle in on your favorites, but it is good to throw in something unexpected every now and then. Experiment and see what unexpected effects you discover.

TOOLS

The type of **needle** you use is personal. I have a selection on hand and make my choice depending on the weight of the fabric and whether I am stitching single or multiple layers together or attaching the pieces to a foundation. Generally, I use sturdy needles—sharps, darners, milliner's, and embroidery needles—using a plain sewing needle that is not too long for the preparation stage, but changing to a heavier, longer needle for attaching pieces to the foundation. The needle

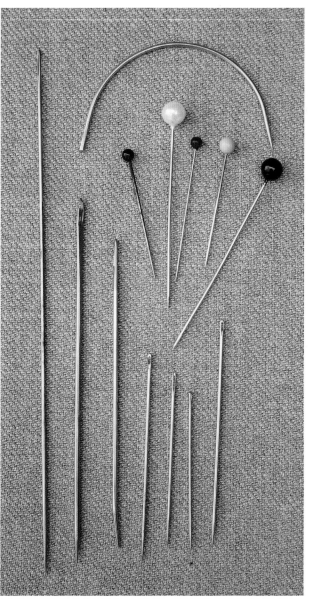

Needles and pins: doll maker's, curved, glover (slightly bent tip), sharps, milliner's and colored pins

needs to take a certain amount of torque, and if it is too thin, the chance of it breaking increases; but too thick, and it may be harder to penetrate through some fabrics.

Some find using a curved needle easier. I find them too thick and less controllable than I like for most projects; however, using them with cut sweater strips was very pleasing. For wide projects, a long doll maker's needle is very helpful.

I highly recommend long **pins** with colored heads. Pins can be easily lost in some of the fabric layers and searching for them is not always a pain-free task.

Pliers are useful to push or pull a recalcitrant needle. Be careful to pull in a straight line with the needle, or you could easily snap it. Keep fingers clear of the point when pushing. A needle grabber might be just as convenient.

I use two types of **thread**: regular cotton sewing thread and a heavy-duty cotton thread. Linen thread is another choice; it is a bit thicker than the thread I use, but many like it. I prefer not to use polyester or nylon thread as a consideration from my antique textile restoration/conservation practice. I feel that the strength of the polyester and nylon thread may cut through or cause abrasion on cotton, silk, linen, or wool fabric. However, if a blended fabric is used, polyester or cotton with polyester core thread would be fine (though I find it tangles easily, so I shy away from it).

Hooking **frames** have gripper bars that will hold fabric tautly, and a project can be easily repositioned. If the foundation fabric is not attachable to your hooking frame, I have found making a stretcher bar frame to be very helpful. Stretcher bars can be purchased from an art supply store in various lengths and are easily assembled. They can be taken apart and reassembled in other sizes for later projects or used to frame your finished piece. If you use a stretcher bar frame, a **stapler and staples** are needed to mount the foundation fabric to it.

I hand cut all my strips, even for hooking, so **scissors** (straight and/or pinking) and a **rotary cutter** and **board** are what I use. The rotary cutter is very good for cutting on the bias. A **strip cutter** might be good, but only for smaller coils, as it is not likely to cut strips wide enough for most of the elements.

General **markers** and **tailor's chalk** come in handy. The chalk marks can be removed if needed. I often sew a running stitch around my design elements so I do not have to worry about unintended marks, and a change in design is easily accommodated.

Stretcher bars

PATTERNS

I start projects with a general idea of which techniques and colors I want to use, but in most every case I end up modifying my original plan as colors and shapes suggest other options. Once you become familiar with these techniques, you will see places they can be used in almost any design. The patterns provided in this book can be used as shown or scaled to a desired size. Do not feel compelled to use the techniques exactly as shown; they are just one of numerous ways each pattern could be done.

Be flexible and willing to alter your plans as new ideas come forward. Let mistakes and accidents lead you to something unexpected.

Planning and Preparation

Before you jump in and start to work on the design, there are a few things to do or keep in mind to help things go more smoothly. The preparation may take a little longer, but it could save you frustrations.

CHOOSE AND PREPARE THE FOUNDATION

If you plan to leave some of the foundation exposed and will not include any hooking, you need a sturdy, attractive fabric, such as medium- to heavy-weight linen, cotton duck, velveteen, canvas, or heavier wool. If you wish to use something lighter, give it more stability with an iron-on fusible. Interfacing alone or a fusible webbing that is pressed between the foundation fabric and a piece of lighter weight cotton will also work well.

If part of the design will be hooked, use whatever hooking foundation you prefer; there is no need to fuse any support to it. The non-hooked elements will be sewn to the hooking foundation. If the project is to be self-supporting, you need no foundation.

CONSIDER FINISHING

How will you use your finished piece; will it be bound, incorporated into something else, or framed? This may determine how much allowance to leave on the edges and whether you want the edges to be cut, torn, bound, or hemmed. I have found that many times I start with one idea and it changes by the time I am finished. Try to leave options open by leaving more allowance than you think you will need.

MARKING/TRANSFERRING THE DESIGN

Measure out the size of your project (keeping the grain straight) and hand sew a running stitch around the outer edge. Now you know where the boundary is and can judge how to position the design elements within the space and not be misled by the edge allowance.

It might be faster to trace or copy the design elements on the foundation with a marker, but before

you do, please consider whether you will be leaving some of the foundation uncovered or if it will be covered completely with other fabric. If you are working your design on a hooking foundation and fabric will cover the entire foundation, then mark away as the design lines will be covered. However, if you plan to leave any part of the foundation exposed, please do not use a marker. Invariably you will find your design will change, the proportions will vary, and you will be stuck trying to figure out how to cover those exposed markings. It is safer to stitch a running line around the design elements.

ABOVE: Design drawn on tissue paper and pinned to foundation TOP RIGHT: Design stitched through tissue and foundation, with tissue partially torn off BOTTOM RIGHT: Stitched outline of the design on foundation

I use two ways to transfer and mark the design with stitches. One is to cut out templates of the design elements, move them around in various positions until I'm satisfied, pin them in place on the foundation, and sew a running stitch around them. This works well if you want to use the elements in a different arrangement than the given pattern.

The other is to trace the design on tissue paper, pin the tissue as a whole to the foundation, and sew a running stitch to outline the design lines through the tissue and foundation. Use a thread color different from the foundation and different from what you will be using to fasten the fabric elements. Once all the outline stitching is done, tear away the tissue paper, taking care not to pull on the stitches. When the work is done, the outline stitches, if they are still visible, can be easily removed (especially if you used a different thread color). You do not want to end up cutting threads that are holding your elements in place.

MOUNT ON A FRAME

Working on a frame will keep the stitches holding the elements from pulling and distorting the foundation fabric. Once your pattern has been transferred to the foundation fabric, use stretcher bars or a hooking frame to hold the work.

If the foundation fabric does not stay on grippers or is too small for your hooking frame, cut a piece of fleece to stretch over the grippers. Cut out the center section, leaving about 2" (5 cm) within the hooking frame. Pin or temporarily stitch the smaller fabric to the fleece and stretch over the grippers. Be sure the design section of the fabric is clear of any other fabric;

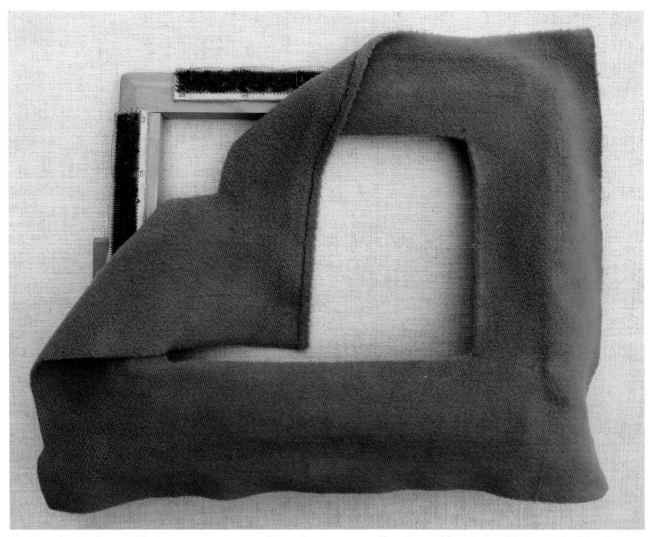

A piece of polar fleece with the center cut out can be used to secure smaller pieces of foundation fabric on a hooking frame for ease of handling.

you do not want to inadvertently sew the hooking frame fabric to your foundation fabric.

If you wish to use a separate frame, one is easily made with stretcher bars, and the foundation fabric can be temporarily stapled to the frame. For the patterns in this book, when not using a hooking frame, I used four 11" (22.9 cm) stretcher bars, which provide an interior space of 8" x 8" (20.3 cm x 20.3 cm), the pattern size. In hindsight, I wish I had used a larger frame, as it can be difficult to stitch close to the inner frame edge. Also, the foundation fabric may stretch a bit when mounting it on the stretcher bars. Adjusting for that, I stapled the fabric slightly off center and repositioned it when I came to work on the other edges.

Staple the foundation fabric to the frame, making sure it is taut. To keep it fairly square, I staple opposing corners first (i.e., right and left sides), pulling the fabric taut. Then I staple the fabric in the middle of those stretcher bars. Make sure the weave of the foundation fabric is straight with the edge of the frame. Proceed with the other opposing sides and add any other staples needed to keep it square and tight.

If you prefer to work without a frame, pull the foundation back to square after every few stitches, as it is easy for the foundation to get puckered and misshapen. Of course, if you are working without a foundation, frames are not needed, and you may find working on a table or your lap most convenient.

CHAPTER 3

Techniques

Preparing the Fabric

CUTTING ON THE STRAIGHT

You can get narrower strips if you cut rather than tear the fabric; generally I do not go narrower than $1/4$" (.6 cm) as the strips can become hard to handle if they are narrower. Cut strips have a clean edge, the color is sharper, and the edge threads are more easily seen. If you cut by hand, it may take longer, but you can cut more exactly along a thread line (though it is not always easy to follow a thread line and width may still vary slightly). It is faster with a strip cutter, and the width is consistent, but the cut may not be exactly along a thread line, the width will be too narrow for most of these techniques except the coiling method, and the coils will be very small. A rotary cutter is another option.

Fabric that is cut may unravel, so using well-fulled fabric or a fabric that does not unravel is easier to handle.

Many fabrics have a different warp and weft threads; cutting the fabric perpendicular or parallel to the selvage will show how they change. The variations will be most noticeable with fabrics that have a different colored warp and weft threads and with plaids.

CUTTING ON THE BIAS

Any fabric can be cut on the bias and there is no worry of unraveling as there is with strips cut on the straight (other than on the ends, but they can be cut off square—perpendicular to the bias cut). Fabric not especially suitable for cutting on the straight or tearing can be cut on the bias with great results. Cutting by hand or with a rotary cutter is easy, and if the cuts are slightly off the 45° line, it does not matter. As you cut into a corner of fabric you will get shorter strips; these can be overlapped with other strips to extend

Warp and weft variations from the same fabric, torn, cut, and on the bias

Bias strips cut into corners can be used; even the smallest piece can be used in a bundle.

them. Do not make the strips too narrow, or they will come apart if pulled.

An interesting variation would be to cut strips with pinking shears, which could be used in any of the techniques.

TEARING

Torn strips will be on the straight of the grain and the width uniform for the length of the strip. They may have fuzzy edges, so color and threads are not as sharp as with cut edges. Some edges may be too fuzzy, but can be trimmed if needed. The narrowest I am able to tear a piece without it coming apart or distorting is $1/2$" (1.3 cm), and even then not all fabrics will easily tear that narrow. Some fabrics will tear crosswise and lengthwise, some just crosswise, and others do not tear well at all.

Preparing the Elements

Elements should fit just inside pattern outlines, or the design may become distorted.

SHIRRING

The basic definition of shirring is the manipulation of fabric by gathering threads. You may be familiar with the term as it is used in clothing, where two or more parallel rows of stitching are pulled to contour fabric in fitting a garment rather than using darts or pleats. Shirring is also the first step in smocking, as found in girls' dresses. The shirring described here is gathered as well, some with only one thread along a narrow strip of fabric, and others as a means to hold fabric in a manipulated shape.

Shirring is a most versatile technique and can be used to great effect with all types of fabric, from thin to thick, including many that are not always suitable for hooking.

These are the basic forms of shirring; keep in mind there are a multitude of variables in this technique. The type of fabric used and variation in assembly will give a distinctive look to each piece. Some of these descriptions can easily be seen as crossing over into the standing wool category. The intent is not to define these techniques with hard delineations, but to explore their possibilities.

Bias shirring is made with strips of fabric cut on the bias, generally $3/4$"–2" (1.9 cm–5 cm) wide. Wider cuts are fine, but realize that the finished strip width will be half the cut width when folded. Too narrow—$3/4$" (1.9 cm) is the narrowest I go—and it will be difficult

Prepared strips (left to right): straight of the grain-cut blanket-weight fabric gathered heavily; torn skirt-weight fabric gathered slightly; bias-cut plaid skirt-weight fabric gathered slightly; bias-cut hound's-tooth check fabric; bias-cut solid fabric; bias-cut shirt-weight fabric; bias-cut challis-weight fabric; bias-cut plaid coarse-weight antique wool

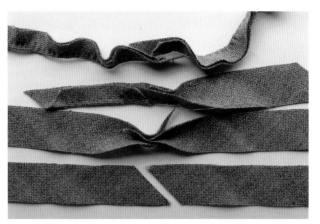

Overlapping bias-cut strips, from bottom up: Be sure angles are aligned, then overlapped and pinned. They can be sewn as one piece, or two separate pieces can be overlapped when you attach them to the foundation.

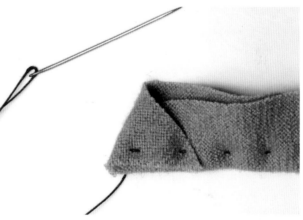

To avoid raw ends, fold the end of a bias strip back and secure it in the stitching.

to handle; too wide and it might not hold its form well. The strips are folded in half lengthwise and held folded with a running stitch close to the fold. How many stitches per inch is a personal choice; you will find what suits you best. The weight of the fabric will also influence your stitches; with thinner fabric you can make smaller stitches than with thicker fabric. This running stitch can be pulled up slightly to accentuate the ripples that will naturally occur with bias-cut fabric.

Join strips by overlapping ends as you sew the folded strips together, or lap them side by side as you sew them to the foundation. I prefer lapping them as I sew them to the foundation, since cutting a strip will cause it to undo a bit and it is easier to add in shorter pieces than fix a cut strip.

Use heavy-duty thread to sew the folded edge to the foundation with stitches about 1"–1^1/$_2$" (2.5 cm–3.8 cm) apart, shaping, coiling, or overlapping as you follow your design. Subsequent strips are sewn ^{1}/$_2$"–1" (1.3 cm–2.5 cm) from the previous strip, though very thin fabric may need to be sewn closer. The thicker the fabric, the farther apart strips can be sewn. Do not worry about lining up the ripples with the previous strip's ripples, as they do it on their own—and if they vary it provides a nice effect, too.

If you do not want a raw end on your bias strip, or if the strip will start or end on an edge, fold the end of a prepared strip over, bringing the raw end even with the folded edge. Stitch it in with the stitching used to hold the fold together.

The bias strips can be made in a single layer folded or in two or three layers stacked together, then folded

Sample swatches torn and sewn to a foundation. Though short, they are still effective.

RIGHT: Bias-shirred strips can be attached to the foundation singly, as for the horse's mane.

lengthwise and gathered up as if one piece. Each strip can be sewn individually to a foundation, or several strips can be joined together and the unit then stitched to a foundation.

You can attach the bias strips to the foundation without these steps, but from personal experience I can tell you the folded strips are easier to control if they are sewn lengthwise first.

Shirring strips can also be made using strips **torn** or cut on the **straight of the grain**. The look is a bit different, and the risk of unraveling is greater, depending on the fabric used. There is not the natural ripple that occurs in the bias strips, but that can be achieved

by gathering the strip slightly, as in the steps for preparing the bias strips already discussed.

Compared to bias strips, straight-of-the-grain strips are easier to attach directly to the foundation without folding and stitching first, especially if the strips are shorter.

Several of the antique rugs I have seen appear to be made by attaching the strips directly to the foundation with a running stitch down the center of the strip. It is then folded to the side, another strip is laid in beside it and attached down the center, and so on. It has occurred to me that this may be more easily done if one works without a frame, as the foundation fabric

Various forms of fringed shirring, both coiled and straight. Three (lavender/ black, purple/yellow, and rust) are fringed with the folded edge up; two have a single layer of another color inserted in the fold; and all have been coiled. Three (gray, red/brown, and red/yellow) are fringed with the raw edge up. They are coiled, with one strip of red wool coiled around the base. Three other fringed strips are sewn in rows rather than coiled; one is cut with the raw edge up (pink), another is torn and unraveled a bit (brown), and one has its folded edge up (multicolored).

would roll away, making it easier to hold the attached strip off to the side while the next strip was added on, but I have not tried it that way.

Fringed shirring is yet another variation, made with strips torn or cut on the straight of the grain. This is best done with densely woven or felted material. Be sure the strip is wide enough—at least 1" (2.5 cm)—to make the fringe long enough to achieve the desired effect. Snip three quarters of the way through the strip perpendicular to the edge, roll the strip, and secure.

Another method is to use a strip twice the width desired, fold it in half lengthwise, and stitch it together as for the shirring above, either on the folded side or the raw edge. If sewn along the raw edges, the folded edge becomes the fringed top. For added interest, insert a single strip of fabric of a contrasting color between the folded strip, and stitch the three layers together, either raw edge or folded edge up. Once stitched, carefully snip small cuts along the length and

Chenille strips made with various fabrics, both cut and torn. Top row, left to right: bias-cut silk, bias-cut polyester, torn skirt-weight wool, bias-cut shirt-weight wool, bias-cut shirt-weight wool. Bottom row, left to right: bias-cut cotton, bias-cut polyester, torn very light-weight wool, bias-cut skirt-weight wool (gathered but not twisted so individual pleats are seen more clearly), bias-cut challis-weight wool.

Hiding the Knot

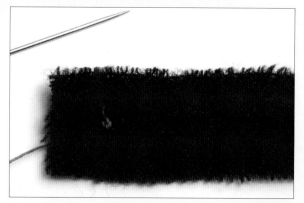

To hide the knot, place it as in this photo.

Fold the end over the knot and proceed to run the gathering stitch down the center.

Before you get to the end of the strip, fold the end in and stitch through the fold. Gather the strip to desired density, take a few small stitches in the end gathers, then run the needle about an inch (2.5 cm) back into the chenille strip and cut the thread.

use the strip coiled, folded, or straight. When rolled, the inner strip will peek out through the folded loop fringe.

Chenille shirring creates a rounded strip reminiscent of a caterpillar, hence the name. It is made with bias-cut strips or with straight-of-the-grain strips that have been torn or cut. Keep in mind that some fabrics do not tear in narrow strips, and if the fabric unravels easily, it can become unsightly, with lots of threads hanging loose (unless that appearance is desired, as it can make a dramatic statement).

Make the strips, whether bias or straight of grain, approximately $3/8"-5/8"$ (1 cm–1.6 cm) wide. If the bias-cut fabric is too narrow, the strip may come apart, and if too wide, the fabric may not gather up properly.

Using heavy-duty thread, hand sew a running stitch down the center of the strip, gather it up firmly and fully (be careful not to pull so much as to cause the thread to break), and secure. This form works well with thinner fabrics, as they gather easily; thicker fabrics may not gather enough to make the distinctive caterpillar form, but the effect can still be desirable. After it is gathered and secured, you sometimes need to twist the strip to get it looking "caterpillary."

If your strip is long, gather it up partly and secure with a backstitch before doing the next section. I sometimes prefer to make shorter pieces, because cutting a chenille strip in mid-attachment will cause the piece to come undone. The short pieces can be added to the foundation easily and invisibly by butting ends.

Attach the chenille strips to the foundation by sewing into the strip well enough so any use will not cause the fabric to pull out, but such that the sewing thread is not seen. The stitches will be about 1"–2" (2.5 cm–5 cm) apart. The strip can be gathered loosely for a different effect. Experimentation can lead to interesting results!

Bundled shirring makes the most of small pieces of fabric or short leftover hooking strips. For bundles of yarn or hooking strips, collect 4 to 6 pieces (depending on the thickness of the fabric) that are about 2"–3" (5 cm–7.6 cm) long, keeping in mind that the height of the finished bundle will be half the length of the strips. Stitch through the center point of each strip, fold the bundle in half (the ends double), and stitch through the folded area to secure or wrap the thread tightly just above the fold and secure it.

Each bundle will be sewn to the foundation. How closely you sew them will depend on how thick your fabric is and how densely you want the surface to be covered. You will not get much detail from this form,

Chenille strip of raw silk, cut ¹/₄" (.6 cm) wide, twisted and not yet twisted

BELOW: *For a dimensional effect, attach the end of a chenille strip, loop it up, and secure the other end of the strip to the first end. If your strip is long, make a series of loops that are secured to the foundation.*

Bundled fringe: The top row shows the steps of assembly, and the bottom row shows looped, slant-cut ends, and round-cut ends.

but it yields a very soft, lush surface. They are also nice mixed in as small details or accents. The ends can be left blunt cut, slant cut, or rounded off for more variation.

Fabric shapes—round, square, narrow oblong, or whatever shape you wish to play with—can be folded in a variety of configurations. The simplest is folded in half, then in quarters. As for all of these variations, stitch through and around the fold point to secure the form and sew them to the foundation.

Circles and squares can also be folded in half, then in thirds, making a nice funnel-shaped bud, or simply folded in half and rolled. Rolling a folded piece of fabric gives a different effect than rolling two cut pieces together.

Cutting into a circle, about three quarters of the way through, and wrapping the cut side around a coil makes an interesting shape. Add several and vary the size of the coil for various effects. If trying this with a square, the results are better when the cut is made diagonally from a corner rather than along a flat side. How you stitch these sliced shapes to the coil can also influence the shape.

Fold in half oblong pieces ³/₄" x 2" (1.9 cm x 5 cm), then fan the ends off center from each other. Fold them in half lengthwise and secure. Again, the ends can be cut blunt, slanted, or rounded.

Let no scrap go to waste; a variety of fabrics combined give interesting results.

Pleated shirring was the fussiest and least satisfying for me to work with. However, there is something pleasing and calming about a pleated surface.

Cut or tear strips on the straight of grain approximately ³/₄"–1¹/₂" (1.9 cm x 3.8 cm) wide, though the width of the strip is only limited by ease of handling and desired effect. I can think of no reason that this would not work with bias-cut strips, though I have not tried it. This technique works well for thicker wool,

Round bundling done two ways: First, folded, pinked, and wrapped around a fringed bundle. Second, two circles wrapped around a coil, with a bead in the center.

BELOW: Various ways of square bundling: Folded in on itself, folded and rolled around a fringed bundle, or cut into two squares from the corner and wrapped around a coil with a fringed bundle in the center.

Squares and circles folded and rolled have interesting shapes.

When wrapping cut circles or squares around coils, add a stitch at the inside of the cut to get the fabric to fold up, otherwise it does not look as nice.

RIGHT: Oblong short strips with rounded or slant-cut ends make nice elements when folded singly or in pairs.

This pleated leaf and flower look better with thicker fabric, as the pleats hold their shape.

This pleated border is made with thin wool and the pleats do not have structural integrity as they would with thicker wool.

The end of a pleating strip is sewn down and the strip is flipped over to hide the raw end. The pleating continues to the left.

as it has the body to stand up, whereas a thinner fabric might be too limp unless it is very densely pleated.

Attach the width of the strip to the foundation, loop the strip up to make a pleat, and again sew across the width to attach it to the foundation. How closely the pleats are sewn depends on the thickness of the fabric. Leave the beginning and end of the strip shorter than the height of the pleats, as the pleats will hide the raw ends of the strips. It is likely that you do not need to sew them as closely as you think, since the top pleat loop fills in the space. If sewn too closely, the fabric will become jammed together, and it will be harder and harder to sew the pleats.

If starting on an edge, sew the first width with the fabric end on the inside of the design, then flip the strip over the top and proceed; this will cover the short end. If ending on an edge, turn the last pleat end to the inside and attach to the foundation.

Eyeballing the height of the strips as I sewed was not satisfying; they were more uneven than I wanted. Next, I measured and marked the spacing on the strips with a tailor's marking pencil. If you mark, keep in mind that you want to mark the section of the pleat that is sewn to the foundation, as that will not be seen. Remember that the height of the pleat will be half what you measure between markings. I resorted to sewing running stitches as markers on the pleating strip, as the tailor's chalk had a tendency to rub off.

Pleating is easiest with straight lines or gradually curving designs. If you want to make a shape within the pleat, the strip must be tapered. Figuring out what shape to make the fabric to get the design you want depends on the shape you want and the height of the pleats. Making a paper template and pleating it up will help you figure that out, but remember that the paper will take up less room than the fabric when pleated.

Note

There are times when the difference between forms and terminology are vague, overlapping, or conflicting, or where people from various regions use dissimilar definitions; it can become confusing and get in the way. The intent is to explore and discover ways of working with fiber and not get too bogged down by terminology and strict definitions. These are all wonderful ways of working fabric to aesthetic ends.

Making a Leaf

I spent more time than was reasonable trying various ways to make a template for a pleated leaf, none of them yielding a shape I liked. Finally, I decided to pin pleat a strip of fabric in place, cut out a paper pattern, mark the pattern on the pin-pleated fabric with stitches, undo the pins, and see what shape came out. A lot of work for a simple shape and maybe why there are very few antique examples of pleated rugs!

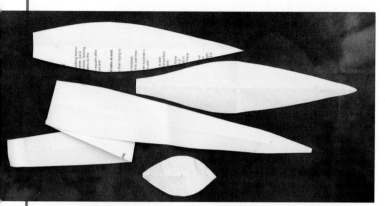

Paper templates for pleating are matched to the sewn pleated pieces in the photo below. The small dark leaf template measured 1¼" (3.2 cm) at the end, 2½" (6.4 cm) at the widest, and 10½" (26.7 cm) long. It made a leaf 2½" (6.4 cm) long. The small lighter leaf template measured ¾" (1.9 cm) at the end, 2½" (6.4 cm) at the widest, and 12" (30.5 cm) long. It made a leaf 3¾" (9.5 cm) long. The large dark leaf template measured 1¼" (3.2 cm) at the end, 2½" (6.4 cm) at the widest, and 25" (63.5 cm) long. It made a leaf 5¾" (14.6 cm) long. The small leaf paper template was the pattern I wanted my leaf to be when I used the pin-pleating method.

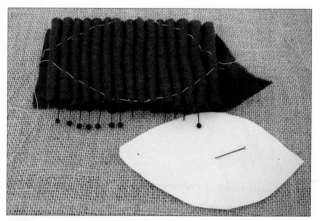

Pinned pleats with thread stitched through the top of each pleat make a template outline. Make sure you leave very long threads or they will pull out of the pleats after you unpin it and pull it flat. Paper pattern is 2⅛" (5.4 cm) wide and 4" (10.2 cm) long.

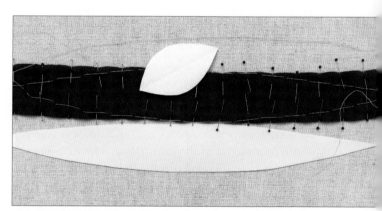

This is the pin-pleated leaf pattern unpinned and pulled flat. Reinsert the pins to mark the spacing of the pleats. The template on the next page is made from following the thread lines, 2⅛" (5.4 cm) at the widest point and 18" (45.7 cm) long. The original leaf shape pattern is at the top.

Pleated leaves on linen from paper templates in photo at top. None of them was a satisfying shape.

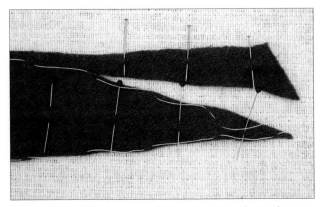

Cut excess fabric away following the thread lines. Place pins within the pleat strip, not on the edge. Red pins mark stitch lines on the leaf shape; regular pins are on the scrap piece.

I pulled the threads out and began to stitch the pleating strip in place, stitching the first line so I could flip the strip over and not have a blunt end exposed.

Once all the pleats were sewn, it was fairly close in size and shape to my original desired pattern. Now that there was a template from my pattern, subsequent leaves proceeded much more quickly. Whew! As you can see, pleating uses a lot of fabric.

Pleated leaf is nearly done; there is one pleat left, and the last one has its end folded to the inside to hide the raw end.

The pleated leaf is complete and is shown with the paper pattern for the original leaf design.

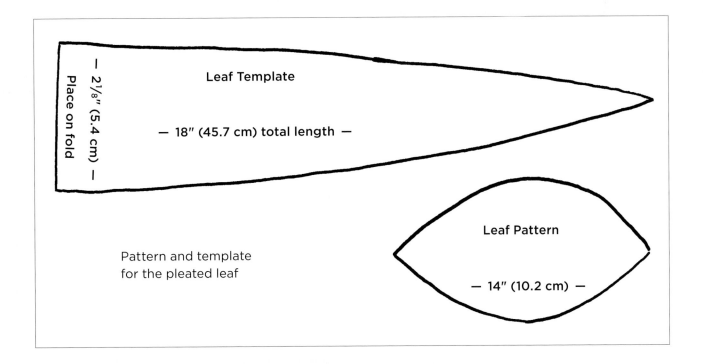

Leaf Template

— 2¹⁄₈" (5.4 cm) —
Place on fold

— 18" (45.7 cm) total length —

Pattern and template for the pleated leaf

Leaf Pattern

— 14" (10.2 cm) —

Yet another method is to attach the fabric pleating strip to the foundation following a stitched or marked design and cut the pleating strip to shape as you go. On one level this may seem to be the easiest, but it means that every pleated element is re-created each time. That is fine if only a few pleated pieces are used, but much more exhausting if there are many.

The difference I make between pleated shirring and standing wool pleating is the pleated shirred strip has folds sewn down on the foundation, while the standing wool pleated strips are sideways with the edges up and down, whether they are sewn to a foundation or to other strips and are self-supporting.

STANDING WOOL

Standing wool is a term that can be used to describe a variety of techniques. I first came across the term used with strips of wool sewn to each other and "standing" without the need of a foundation. These strips were either pleated sideways or bunched, much like chenille shirring though not as densely gathered. They could also be lengthwise-folded strips of wool, with the fold up or down, arranged in coiled and/or undulating patterns. The term seems to have expanded into foundation work when it is "standing" up in strips that have been coiled or wrapped in patterns folded back and forth.

The fabric strips are generally $1/2$"–4" (1.3 cm–10 cm) wide. Those wider than 2" (5 cm) may be folded in half lengthwise. They can be torn or cut. If the edges are exposed (for pieces not folded lengthwise), there may be some threads that come undone with use; these can be snipped off and will diminish with time.

The fabric used for this technique can be any type, not just wool; but, generally, standing wool fabric is a thicker, firmer fabric, such as blanket or coat wool, especially if it is being used without a foundation. If a foundation is used, a sturdier foundation fabric is better to support the weight.

In this technique, stronger thread and longer, sturdier, and/or curved needles would come in handy. Each strip can be sewn down the middle and gathered, as in chenille shirring, then wrapped or coiled in a pattern and sewn to the strip next to it. If the strips are folded lengthwise, they are stitched through the sides to the next row of strips in various patterns. Many arrangements include coiled pieces of wool as well. Some strips are folded and sewn to the adjoining strips or coils as you go, with no need to prepare them.

Each design layer, or round, is sewn to the next with internal stitches, and various design layers can be arranged as desired. To maintain stability and durability, it is important that the stitches holding the design elements to one another are not too widely spaced and that each strip, fold, and coil is secured snugly to the strip, fold, or coil next to it.

When adding on new strips, stagger the ends and overlap them so there are no strip ends in the same place on subsequent rounds or layers.

One of the best things about standing wool is that you can keep adding on to the design as you go along. A plan is not necessary; the arrangement of the elements can be decided as you go as well. A small rug or mat can grow spontaneously and substantially with time.

Instead of sewing, some makers assemble their standing wool pieces using fabric glue or hot glue. Please pretest the glue to be sure that it is compatible with the fabric you are using. Do not use hot glue with polar fleece or synthetics, as they may melt—take precautions to prevent burning your fingers.

COILING

Coiling is an element of standing wool, but it is distinctive enough to have its own name. In fact, it is known by several names, such as spools, scrolls, rolls, and beads. However, it is most often called a quillie. In this book, I have used the descriptive terms *coiling* and *coil* for continuity, but recognize that the term *quillie* is quite common.

Coils are made from fabric strips that are generally between $1/4$" and 2" (1.3 cm and 5 cm) wide. Wider can be made, and of course the type of fabric makes a difference. Narrow strips are better for making small coils, but they will become unstable if the coils are made too large, and the center may fall out. Using strips of fulled sweaters can yield wonderful results. It is also a great way to put short hooking strips and odd bits of fabric to use.

The fun of making coiled pieces is multidimensional. One can use up hooking leftovers; a wide variety of fabrics can be used, giving countless effects; the coils can be inserted into other techniques to

> **Tip**
>
> Coiling is a great way to make use of idle time. Mix colors from other projects. Introduce a common color to tie disparate strips together, and use up very short pieces.

Pieces too small for hooking, such as swatch samples, are cut and coiled.

embellish, adding interest and texture; and the technique is easily adaptable to make small pieces, such as pins or trivets, or much larger pieces, such as rugs or installation exhibits.

The strips are rolled, wrapped, or coiled around until they are of a desired diameter, and then secured. They can be made with single strips or with double, or even triple, strips coiled simultaneously. The shorter the coiling strips and the more of them coiled at once, the fussier it is, but it can be well worth the visual effects.

Use a heavier thread to secure the coils, and you may find that a long doll-making or curved needle will come in handy for the stitching. I have used glue on fabric (denim and dense felt) that was too difficult to pierce with a needle. The coils are sewn to a sturdy foundation or to each other.

Depending on the effect you want, the width of the strip need not be consistent throughout the coil, but for most an even width works best. Roll each strip with your fingers; it may take a little practice to get used to starting each strip, but pinching it with your fingernails will help hold it until the coil is larger and easier to handle. If the strip width varies, as mine do since I hand cut my strips, I like to make sure one side of the coil is consistently even and level.

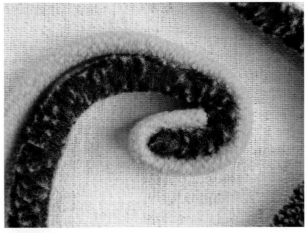

To start a coil with two strips, wrap the end of one around the other, then begin wrapping. This will give a balanced color arrangement.

If the strips are fairly wide, coils can be started with your fingers and then rolled quickly along your thigh or palm. How tightly you coil the strips depends on your fabric and how you plan to use the finished pieces. Most of mine are wrapped firmly, but not too tightly. If you are using bias-cut fabric strips, sweaters, or anything that has a lot of stretch, do not wrap them too tightly, as you do not want to distort the fabric or risk pulling the strip apart.

There are various ways of joining strips in coils. Left to right, wrap two strips together simultaneously; start with one color and add in another, wrapping them together; wrap one color, then start another color with ends butted up to keep coil round.

It's better to use decorative pins as these plain pins were easily lost in the work.

When rolling two strips together simultaneously, start with the end of one strip folded over the end of the other strip. Join in a new strip by butting the ends together; keep tension even and roll until you reach the end or another strip is added on. It may take a bit of practice to hold the rolled part secure and join in the next strip tightly enough, especially if the strips are not very long. Strip sections can be added on at any time to achieve the look and coloration design you want.

After each coil is rolled or wrapped, it is secured with stitches or glue, and then joined to others or to a foundation. The only case where I did not secure each coil after it was rolled was with the "beaded" necklaces you will see on page 60.

For most coils, only a couple of stitches through the coil will be needed to hold it in shape. Larger coils or some that are very thick may need more. The stitches that will attach the coils to the foundation or to other coils will also hold it together and provide better support.

Some may decide to skip this step with fine results. I find it easier to handle the stitched coils rather than those that are just pinned together, but I fully understand the desire to get started assembling.

For some projects, it is easier to make small units and then join them into larger ones; for other projects, adding coils singly works well. The coils can also be strung on a thread and arranged before securing. This method is suggested by Diana Blake Gray and is

When joining two coils, they look better if the ends are "nested" together. Notice how new strips are added within coils, either butted (right) or laid in (left).

Six Steps to Secure a Coil

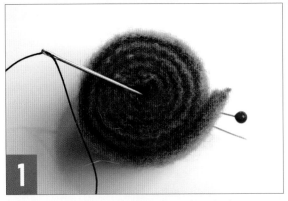

1 To secure each coil after forming it, insert the needle in the center of the coil bottom, passing through the layers of fabric to bring it out at the end of the outside strip.

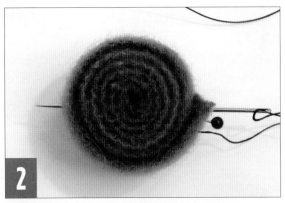

2 Reinsert the needle and push it across through all the layers to the opposite side from the end of the strip.

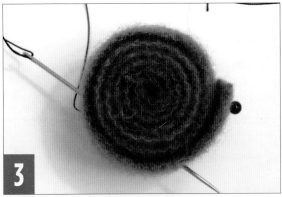

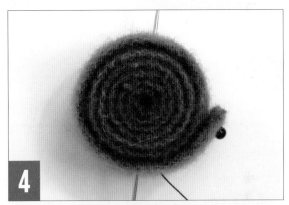

3 **4** Pull it out and reinsert it, passing through a few layers to go a quarter of the way around the coil, and then bring it out and reinsert it again, passing through all the layers and the center to push it out the opposite side.

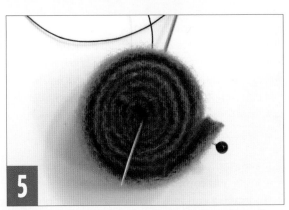

5 Reinsert and push it back to the center of the bottom.

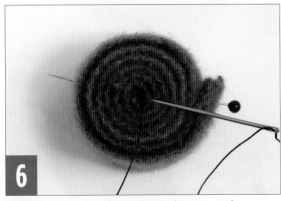

6 Make a couple of small stitches, run the needle to the outside of the coil, and cut the thread. You will have made a cross through the interior of the coil.

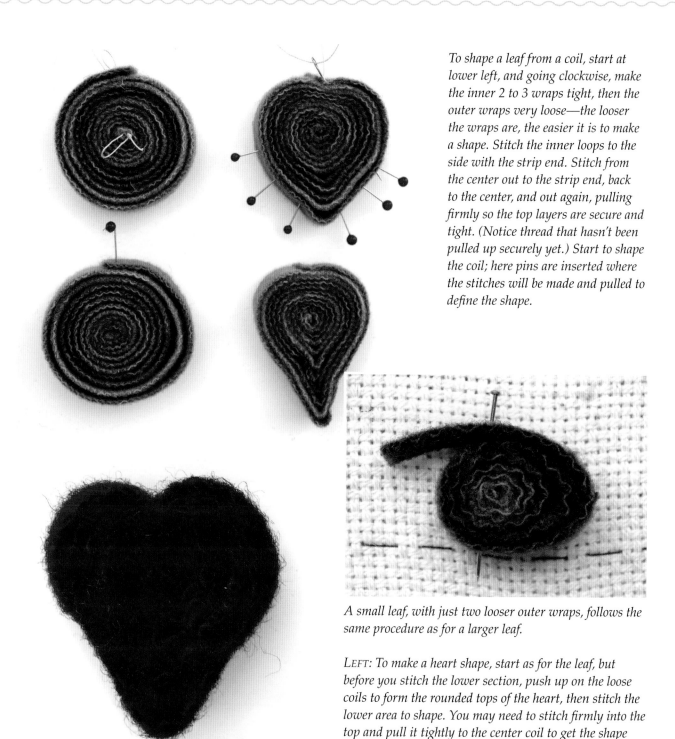

To shape a leaf from a coil, start at lower left, and going clockwise, make the inner 2 to 3 wraps tight, then the outer wraps very loose—the looser the wraps are, the easier it is to make a shape. Stitch the inner loops to the side with the strip end. Stitch from the center out to the strip end, back to the center, and out again, pulling firmly so the top layers are secure and tight. (Notice thread that hasn't been pulled up securely yet.) Start to shape the coil; here pins are inserted where the stitches will be made and pulled to define the shape.

A small leaf, with just two looser outer wraps, follows the same procedure as for a larger leaf.

LEFT: To make a heart shape, start as for the leaf, but before you stitch the lower section, push up on the loose coils to form the rounded tops of the heart, then stitch the lower area to shape. You may need to stitch firmly into the top and pull it tightly to the center coil to get the shape you want.

very helpful to keep the "beads" from rolling away. To ensure even spacing when working a symmetrical design, set the elements opposite each other and fill in between.

To keep a foundation from showing when you add coils to a project and do not fill in right next to them, appliqué a piece of fabric, similar to the color of the coils to be attached, on the foundation, then sew the

coils on top. The fabric will cover the spaces between the coils and foundation.

To make a coil in a form other than round, squeeze the coil to the desired form and stitch it to hold the shape. The shape can also be adjusted when it is attached to the foundation by the other elements sewn or hooked next to it. For shapes that are more extreme, such as a teardrop or leaf, make the outer coils looser

There are other ideas, suggestions, and tips in the Patterns and Projects sections that may be of use. Be sure to check those out even if you do not plan to make the pattern or project shown.

ATTACHING COILS TO THE FOUNDATION

Bring your knotted thread through the foundation (you may want to take a few small stitches so the knot doesn't pull through) in the middle of where your coil will be, insert the needle in the center of the coil and—angling it through all the layers—come out about halfway up on the outside of the coil. Slide the coil to the foundation and insert the needle back in the foundation next to the coil. Bring the needle through the foundation along the edge of the coil about a quarter way around. Halfway up the coil insert the needle and angle it through the layers back toward the middle and go through the foundation. Pull the thread up on the outside edge of the coil across from the second stitch, insert it about halfway up the side of the outer layer of the coil, and angle it through the layers again to the middle (it does not have to be exactly in the middle) and repeat at the point opposite the first stitch. Either secure with a few stitches or, if the thread is long enough and the coils are close enough, pull the thread out in the center of where the next coil will be placed and repeat.

If the coils are small, you may only need three stitches per coil; if quite large, more would be necessary.

If you do not want the stitches to show on the outside of the coil, you will have to get a bit fussy to make sure the needle does not come all the way through that outside coil wrap.

Sewing fabric under the coils will keep the foundation from showing through the gaps if other elements will not hide the foundation.

on one side and pull in the stitches to form and hold the shape; the looser coils allow it to be shaped more easily.

Wool strip wrapped around the center coil shows stitches attaching it to the foundation.

DECORATIVE ATTACHMENT

Another idea is to use the attaching stitches decoratively. Using yarn or embroidery floss, come up through the center of the coil and insert the needle through the foundation at the coil edge. Pull the thread up at the edge of the coil a quarter of the way around and through the center of the coil; repeat as many times as you wish.

Decorative attachment of a coil, finished.

First stitch of decorative attachment of a coil.

Second stitch of decorative attachment of a coil.

CHAPTER 4

Patterns

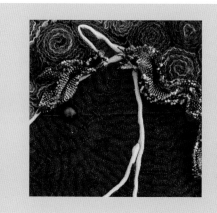  

The instructions for these patterns will tell you how I made them and the materials I used. They are meant as a guide; please adapt them with your own choices of scale, size, and arrangement of color, material, and techniques.

Most of the patterns are small, only 8" x 8" (20.3 cm x 20.3 cm). *The Snow Family Sampler* started out as an 8" x 8" (20.3 cm x 20.3 cm) snowman, but expanded to show a wider variety of techniques. Both the smaller and expanded size patterns are provided.

For the basic how-tos, suggestions, and hints, see Chapter 2—Getting Started. Anything done specifically and only for one pattern will be shown within that pattern's instructions. I have not given many measurements for the making of the shirring, coiling, or standing wool elements; your pattern size, arrangement, and materials will likely be different from what I have done.

Much of the fun and joy comes from using a variety of materials and techniques to see how they turn out. Experiment with combinations and see what can happen. Explore and enjoy!

"On Alert" Horse

Finished dimensions: 8" x 8" (20.3 cm x 20.3 cm)

Techniques
Hooking, coiling, bias shirring, and standing wool

Supplies
Scissors or cutter
Threads
Rug hook
Needles—heavier, longer, and/or curved needle, as works best for you
Fabrics—as shown, made with new, repurposed, and antique wool and hooking foundation
Pliers are optional, but sometimes it is easier to pull/push with pliers than fingers.

Since I knew I was going to hook part of this pattern, I used my usual hooking foundation, monk's cloth. Whatever you normally use is fine. I hand cut all my strips and they were in the $1/4$" (.6 cm) range; the bias-shirred mane was cut about 1" (2.5 cm) wide.

As all design lines would be covered, I marked the pattern on the foundation with a permanent marker. The pattern is small, so I mounted it on a frame, though using a regular hooking frame would have been fine too.

Mane and forelock: I used remnants from a piece of old, homespun, plaid wool fabric. Plaids look great in bias shirring, as you see the variety of colors.

For the mane to stand higher in relief than the other elements, cut the bias strip wider than double the height that the hooking will be. Fold it lengthwise and stitch close to the fold, then gather slightly to put some wave in the strips. I usually leave the ends of bias strips angled, unless the fabric unravels easily, in which case they can be cut square. The angled ends of the strips are overlapped as they are attached to the foundation. When coming to the end of the design, fold and secure the ends.

Outline: The blues and reds I chose are very close in value; I wanted something to define their separation better. Picking up on the light color in the plaid, I made seamed cording out of a cream-colored challis-weight wool cut on the bias. Cut bias strips 1" (2.5 cm), which is four times as wide as the finished cording. The hooking strips are about $1/4$" (.6 cm). Fold each long side in to the center and fold in half again. Stitch the folded sides closed, tucking in ends to desired length.

Bias cording will lie better around curves. Attach the cording to design lines along the horse's outline.

The steps to making bias-shirred strips: Fold strip in half lengthwise, run a stitch near the fold, and gather it slightly.

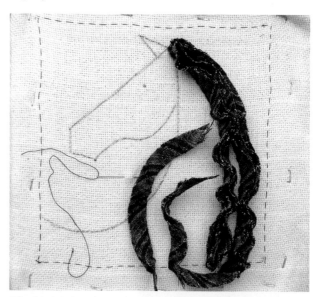

The bias strips are arranged on the pattern; even short strips are used by overlapping them.

Bias piping made from a damaged wool challis shawl. The edges of the strip are folded to the center, then the strip is folded again and sewn closed.

Horse: Hook a selection of reds to fill in the horse. Do not hook too closely to the mane; the bias shirring will expand to fill in any small gaps that appear, as will the next rows of hooking.

The bias-shirred mane and forelock and the outline piping are in place; the hooking has started.

Background: With a selection of blues, make coils of various sizes and combinations and attach them to the foundation along the mane and cording. In oddly shaped areas between the coils, use the strips as standing wool and fold them into spaces and around the coils to make undulating patterns. Attach as you go, and fill in until the background is covered.

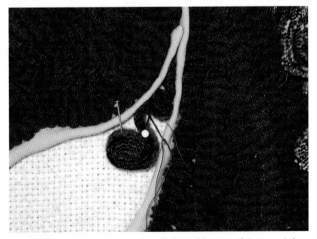

Close-up of a strip of wool coiled and inserted into a tight space

The progress of the coils filling in the background

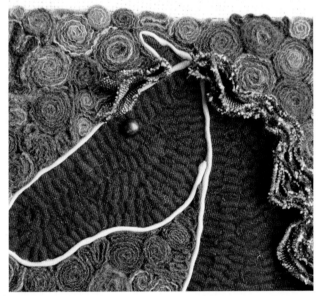

Close-up of wool strips wound around the coils to fill in empty spaces

Binding: Cut or tear strips of wool (I tore them about 2" [5.1 cm] wide) to match the area that the binding will be next to, and sew in place.

This can be made into a pillow or framed.

The binding is sewn to the top before pinning and sewing it to the back. The corners are "boxed" then mitered on the back to make them less bulky.

The back before the binding is folded back and sewn. The corners of the foundation are cut to eliminate more bulk.

Pattern outline

Flower

Finished dimensions: 8" x 8" (20.3 cm x 20.3 cm)

Techniques
Hooking, coiling, standing wool, and chenille shirring

Supplies
- Scissors or cutter
- Threads
- Needles—heavier, longer, and/or curved needle, as works best for you
- Rug hook
- Fabric—as shown, made with wools of varying weights on monk's cloth
- Pliers are optional, but sometimes it is easier to pull/push with pliers than fingers.

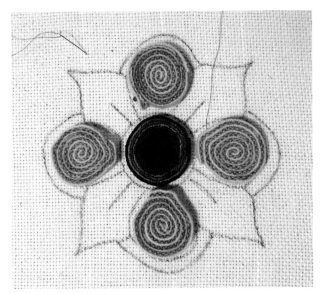

The center coil and three of the petals have been sewn to the foundation. One petal has yet to be shaped, secured, and attached.

Since I knew I was going to hook part of this pattern, I used my usual hooking foundation, monk's cloth. Whatever you normally use is fine. Sew in all center elements and do the hooking last. It is easier to adjust the hooking, even if your project is primarily hooked, than to struggle to fit elements into a space. I hand cut all the strips in the ¼" (.6 cm) range. The turquoise standing wool outline was added after the green was hooked; it is about ¾" (1.9 cm) wide folded in half lengthwise.

As all design lines would be covered, I marked the pattern on the foundation with a permanent marker. The pattern is small, so I mounted it on a stretcher bar frame, though using a regular hooking frame would have worked too.

Decide where to use which techniques, and pick colors keeping in mind contrasts, blending, values, and something to give a bit of punch—in this case the turquoise. Start in the center with the largest elements and work out.

Flower center: Cut strips and wrap coils until desired size. I used several colors, one after another. The final coil wrap is the same as the center color. Secure and attach to the foundation.

Petals: Cut strips from two colors and coil them together simultaneously. Secure the coil and shape the petal to fit the design. Attach to the foundation, but do NOT secure the petals to the flower center. You may also decide to wait until the turquoise strip has been attached before adding the large petals.

The turquoise wool strip wrapped around the center coil shows stitches attaching it to the foundation.

Cut a strip of turquoise wool and wrap it around the flower center and up into each leaf; if it does not show up well enough, wrap it around again. Attach it to the foundation as you go. Attach the petals if you have not already done so.

Wool strips wrap around the petals and end in small coils.

Cut four strips and make a coil at each end. Audition various color options to see whether you want to blend or contrast with what you have already done. You will have to test and see what length works best to get coils the right size. Wrap the middle of the strip around the outside of the petal. Fit the coils between the space at the base of the petal and the turquoise standing wool outline. I added this piece because the petals did not fully fill the pattern lines, and I wanted to add another color and detail rather than make the area all green.

Leaves: To make the leaf shape, make a coil, pinch it on one side, and stitch it securely to hold the teardrop shape. Make four leaf shapes and attach them to the foundation. Use a selection of greens to make coils to fit into the leaf spaces and attach these to the foundation and to each other. As there are likely to be spaces not filled by the coils, use a strip to wind around the coils and fold back on itself to fill in the leaf shapes evenly. Stitch to the foundation and to the previous elements as you go.

A wool strip pinned to make a shaped leaf coil. The outer two coils are much looser so stitches on the right side of the leaf can be pulled tightly to make that end narrower.

Close-up of leaf arrangement

Composition of the leaf shapes and how they fit into the pattern markings

Petal Edges: After completing the leaves, go back to the petals. Cut four strips (I used a very lightweight wool) and make chenille-shirred strips to fill in around the end of the petals. Attach these to the foundation.

The leaves are in place and the chenille-shirred strip is fitted to the space around the top of the petal.

All the flower elements are attached, and the flower is ready for the hooked outline.

Background: Hook two rows around the petals and leaves; this will help hold the flower design in shape. Be careful not to hook the first row too closely to the coils and shirring, or the design may buckle and distort. It may look as if it is not close enough, but the next row of hooking will make any small openings fill in.

Cut a strip of turquoise wool a bit wider than double the width of the hooking strips (this will make it stand up in relief from the hooking). Fold in half lengthwise and attach it to the foundation, being sure to snug it up into the corners of the hooking to maintain the flower design outline.

Hook two more rows around the turquoise and a row at the pattern edge to define the corners. Your color choice will depend on whether you want to blend or contrast with the area next to it. I wanted the center to stand out and yet still be connected to this outer layer, so I used a color that had been used in the center. This leaves a space in each corner. I had planned to hook it all in, but saw a chance to repeat the chenille shirring used on the outside of the petals. Though the colors are similar, it gives a nice textural change without distracting from the flower. Make lengths of chenille shirring and stitch them in place to fill in these spaces.

Strips of chenille shirring are inserted in the corners, between the hooked areas.

Finish this piece with binding, add an extra border of fabric to make it into a pillow, or simply frame it.

The back before the binding is folded over and sewn down

Pattern outline

"An Abundance" Flower Pot

Finished dimensions: 8" x 8" (20.3 cm x 20.3 cm)

Techniques
Hooking, chain stitching, coiling, standing wool, fringed shirring, fringed standing wool, pleating, bundled shirring, and beading

Supplies
Scissors or cutter
Threads
Needles—regular and heavier
Rug hook
Fabric—as shown, made with wools of varying
  weights and cotton knit on monk's cloth

The only flower made before the pot was hooked is the standing wool daisy with a double wool strip around a coil.

Again I began with my usual hooking foundation, monk's cloth, since I would be hooking parts of this design. Whatever you normally use is fine. Attach the floral elements first and do the hooking and chain stitching after that area has been filled in. It is easier to adjust the hooking and chain stitching, even if your project is primarily hooked, than to struggle to fit elements into a space. I hand cut most all the strips in the $1/4$" (.6 cm) range.

As all design lines would be covered, I marked the pattern on the foundation with a permanent marker. In this case, it was only the flower pot that was marked. The pattern is small, so I mounted it on a stretcher bar frame, though using a regular hooking frame would have been good too.

The pattern shows a simple layout of circles, not the floral arrangement that you see in the finished work. I used this piece to show how a variety of techniques might be used. I made many of the elements and then started arranging them to fill the space. When I got to the top, I realized I had run out of room. To end the floral display within the lines would leave it having a squared-off top line—not a look I liked—so why not just expand the flowers over the edge to round out the arrangement?

The only element that intruded into the flower pot was the standing wool daisy with the coiled center. I secured a double loop of petals around the coil and attached it to the foundation, then hooked in the pot. The purple flower only hangs over the edge.

This assortment of various coiled, bundled, and fringed elements—looking more like sushi than flowers— is waiting to be added to the arrangement. The green short strips are bundled, and the orange short strips are bundled and then wrapped in a purple coil. The folded pieces are wool circles in various diameters, $1^1/2$"–2" (3.8 cm–5.1 cm). They have been folded in half and then in half again or folded in half and then in thirds, which makes a funnel shape. The pointed bottom is secured with thread.

Most floral elements have been attached and the hooking and chain stitching is filling in the background.

After most of the elements were attached, I hooked the background in a light blue cotton knit, and chain stitched a beige and cream tweed wool at the bottom.

I made several green fringed bundles to fill in wherever there was a gap; they added nice texture and color without crowding the other elements.

The upper section in preparation for the final elements that will extend beyond the edge. The binding will be sewn on the front of the piece before they are attached.

Chain Stitching

Chain stitching is a crochet stitch (use your rug hook) where a loop is drawn up through the foundation, but the loop stays on the hook as the hook is inserted back through the foundation. The strip underneath is hooked and another loop is drawn up through the foundation and pulled through the loop still on the hook from the previous stitch. This is done across the width. The end of a strip is pulled up through the last loop and then pulled through the foundation to the back to anchor the last loop. The first loop of the next strip is pulled up in the last loop and the process is repeated. Work the loops loosely or the foundation may distort. I used a hooking strip about 1/4" (.6 cm) wide. This leaves short ends on the back.

Detail of the chain-stitched area

To extend the flowers beyond the border, I had to sew in the top side of the binding edge first. In the photo at left, it is pinned in place. This was a time when I hooked the area first and then fit the element into the space. I made a large poppy using a torn strip of heavy wool that had been folded lengthwise and shirred along the fold. It was wrapped around a small black coil, secured, and attached. To the right, you can see the beginnings of what will become a partial daisy-like flower.

Making the last flower to fit in the top section.

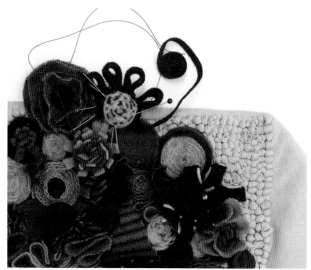

The poppy has been attached and the standing wool flower is being fitted for the remaining space.

With the larger flower attached, the red-petal daisy-like flower is the last to be made. Here (left) it is pinned together to see how it looks and fits. Only one more petal to go and it can be secured and attached to the foundation. A green fringed bundle is used to fill in the final spot. Though the binding has been sewn to the front side, it is not stitched to the back until all the work is done on the front.

Detail of the various buds, flowers, and leaves

This detail of the lower left shows the chain stitching, hooked cotton knit, bound edge, and beaded embellishment on a coil clustered with circle and short-strip bundles.

Pattern outline

The Snow Family Sampler

Finished dimensions: 11" x 14"
(27.9 cm x 35.6 cm)

Techniques

Coiling, standing wool, bias shirring, chenille shirring, bundled shirring, and rolled wool with fabrics that are bias cut, straight cut, and torn

Supplies

Scissors or cutter

Threads

Needles—heavier, longer, and/or curved needle, as works best for you

Fabrics—as shown, this is made with wool and silk

Pliers are optional. Sometimes it is easier to pull/push with pliers than fingers.

This pattern is small, which requires some petite and fussy handwork. Scale the pattern larger and rearrange the elements if you wish.

MR. SNOW

Head: Make a simple single coil of wool. I used strips that were about $^{1}/_{4}$" (.6 cm) wide. Secure the coil and then attach to the foundation.

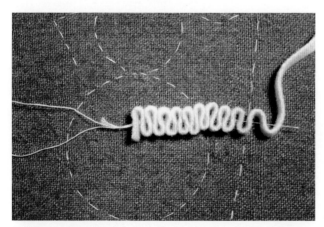

Gathering the strip of wool that will become the middle section

Middle section: Cut a strip of the same wool that you used for the head. With needle and thread, make evenly spaced stitches down the center of the strip lengthwise, gather them up in an undulating line, and join in a circle (standing wool). You may have to try it a few times to get the spacing and loop size you want so it will fit into the design space. Attach it to the

foundation with stitches in the inside and outside of the loops. The buttons are three small coils made with silk from a man's tie that is light gray on one side and blue on the other. Secure them and attach to the foundation. To fill in the remaining space, I used strips of wool, which I curved to fill the open spaces and then attached to the foundation.

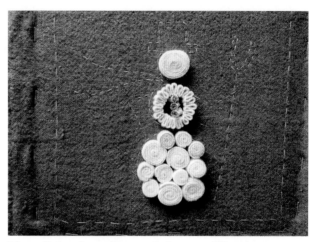

The coiled and standing wool elements filling in on Mr. Snow

Bottom section: Make a selection of coils using a variety of white wools; make smaller coils as needed to fill in gaps. To keep the coils tight, stitch them to each other as well as to the foundation.

Hat: Cut a bias strip of black velvet double the width of the strip used for the head, fold it in half lengthwise, and stitch it to the foundation and to itself if needed to keep it in alignment. To make the hat look like it is not perched on top, either stitch it down on the sides of the head a bit or flatten the head coil on the top. (This fabric was difficult to work with; a chenille-shirred strip of light silk would have been much easier.)

Scarf: Tear a wool strip to desired width of scarf and fold it in half just off center. At the fold, fold it in half lengthwise to place between the head and middle section, and attach it to the foundation. Unravel some of the scarf ends to make fringe and arrange; secure with a few stitches if needed. (In the photos the scarf was made of two separate pieces to eliminate bulk.)

Arms: Cut a double-wide strip of wool to the length desired for the arms. Roll or fold it lengthwise and stitch it closed. Attach to the foundation with the raw edge facing down, making the arms bend as desired.

Broom: Prepare the handle as for the arms; a wool knit was used for this. The broom head is three strips of torn double-wide wool folded lengthwise and attached to the foundation.

Assembling the Scarf

1. Two pieces of wool are arranged for the scarf. **2.** Fold the end that will go at the neck in half lengthwise and stitch it closed, securing both ends together, but only for the length that will fit under the head. **3.** The folded side will fit under the head.

Mr. Snow is nearly finished. More coils are needed so his middle section will not look so precariously balanced on the bottom. You can see the stapling on the frame and extra fabric on the side.

At this point, I realized that there were other techniques that would have worked well, so I decided to make it a family. By good fortune, rather than planning, I had enough extra fabric on my foundation to extend the design frame and add two more family members.

LITTLE SNOW

Head, middle, and bottom section: Make the coils and attach as for the head of Mr. Snow. You can use a single strip of wool or combine two strips and roll them as one for variation in colors.

Cap: Cut a strip of wool and curve it to fit the design. Secure to the foundation either as you go or after you have made the cap. Bring the ends down on the sides of the head to make it sit better. Make a coil for the pom-pom.

Arms: Same as for Mr. Snow.

Finished Little Snow

MRS. SNOW

Head: Make same as the other heads.

Middle section: Make two wool coils for bust and attach in place. Cut bias strip of lightweight silk (width is a bit wider than the coil strip widths), run a stitch down the center and gather up into a fairly dense chenille strip.

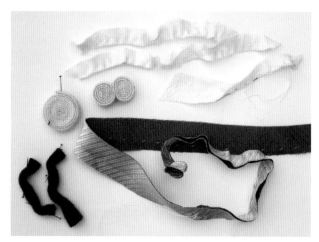

Pieces for Mrs. Snow before assembly: bias-shirred strips for Mrs. Snow's bottom section; white wool; the double-sided silk tie fabric; the head coil and two bust coils; and the rolled arm sections, pinned before sewing

At first I was going to fill in the rest of the middle section with chenille shirring; it would have made for a rather plump Mrs. Snow, but that was okay. However, after I joined the chenille in a circle and attached it between the head and middle section, it dropped down, and I realized that it would make much more interesting arms. The rest of the middle section was filled in with wool strips standing wool fashion, curving back and forth and attached to the foundation at the ends and folds.

Bottom section: Cut silk strips (plain white silk and the same silk used for the buttons on Mr. Snow) twice the desired width. Fold in half lengthwise, stitch close to and along fold, and gather up slightly. Attach to the foundation following the design outline, then fill in as desired. The bottoms of her arms will rest at her waist, where they can be secured.

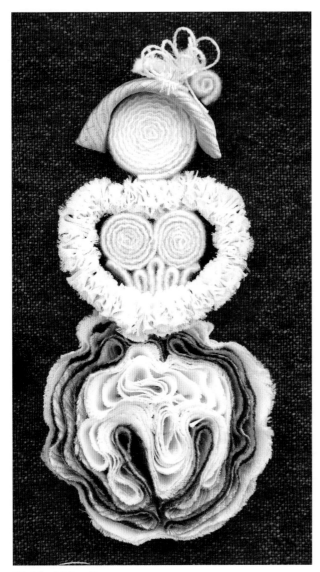

Finished Mrs. Snow

Bonnet: Cut an extra-wide bias strip of silk from the tie, fold in half lengthwise, tucking in the raw edges and the ends, and sew it so the raw edges are hidden. Position it on her head and attach it to the foundation. Make a small wool coil and attach it to the bonnet. Make a small bundle of yarn (this is very thin novelty yarn with glitter in it) or thin hooking strips and attach it at the top of the bonnet. The bonnet could also be made with a bias-shirred strip doubled or tripled over the head or a length of chenille shirring in lighter silk.

Remove outline stitching if seen and prepare for mounting or framing.

If any of the outline stitching show after adding all the elements, very carefully snip the outline threads and remove them. If they extend under the work, pull the snipped ends to the back of the work. It is best to snip them from the front, as you may become confused

as to which threads to snip if done from the back and inadvertently cut a thread holding elements in place. Using a thread color that is different from the foundation and your attaching thread for outlining is helpful.

I gave the wool foundation more substance with fusible interfacing. The color difference happened because I decided to expand the project and could only find the lighter interfacing.

When I finished with the family, I evened off the background fabric, stitched it on linen, and mounted it on a stretcher frame. I decided it was still not quite finished, so I attached small snowballs around the outside, which was an idea I took from Sarah McNamara's *Snowman and Snowballs*. It would have been much easier to sew the snowballs if I had thought of that before mounting it; however, I do like the effect, and it gives it an interesting frame.

Snowball frame detail. The idea for the snowballs came from Sarah McNamara's Snowman and Snowballs.

*Pattern outline of
Mr. Snow*

*Pattern outline of
Little and Mrs. Snow*

Wreath

Finished dimensions: 8¹/₄" x 8¹/₄"
(21 cm x 21 cm) plus cord hanger—made as a hanging ornament (These are the measurements I used; you may find other sizes work better depending on the type of fabric you are using.)

Techniques
Chenille shirring, bias shirring, and coiling

Supplies
Scissors or cutter

Threads

Needles—heavier, longer, and/or curved needle, as works best for you

Pins

Fabrics—as shown, this is made with wool (heavy red felt, challis-weight, and antique paisley) and silk

Pliers are optional. Sometimes it is easier to pull/push with pliers than fingers.

Cut out the paper template and pin it to the foundation of thick red wool felt.

Cut felt about ¹/₄"–³/₈" (.6 cm–1 cm) larger than the template with pinking shears. Cut out the center hole, making the hole smaller by the same measurement.

Mark the design lines on the felt with a running stitch.

Pattern, template, and cut felt with design lines pinned and stitched

Make a selection of ¹/₂" (1.3 cm) bias shirring strips from silk and wool challis by cutting strips 1" (2.5 cm) wide, folding them lengthwise, and stitching close along the fold to hold the folded shape.

Option Layer two or more strips together before folding lengthwise. Cut a strip ¹/₂" (1.3 cm) wide and insert it in the folded wider strip before stitching.

Silk and wool challis bias and chenille strips in the making and coils made from felt and antique paisley

The gathered bias-shirred strips need to be a specific size—a little less than 3" (7.6 cm)—to fit on the design line. Normally I stitch each length of bias shirring as I go, but here I decided it would be better to make each section separately (several strips joined together to make a unit) and then attach them to the foundation.

Clockwise from the top right: bias strips cut and pinned, sewn and slightly gathered, pinned together in desired length, sewn together as a unit, and attached in place standing perpendicular to the felt.

I used several layers of thin silk. I made each unit to fit the design line, overlapping ends or folding them in so there were no loose ends at the sides of the wreath. Stitch the bias strips for each unit together at the folds. Make five (or as many as your design needs) and attach to the foundation following the design lines.

Make several small coils. I used some of the foundation material and combined it with strips from a damaged antique paisley. In some, I included a strip of silk. Attach them to the red felt foundation.

The bias-shirred strips are attached as are the various small coils; time to add the chenille strips.

Make a selection of ¹/₂" (1.3 cm) chenille-shirred strips from various greens of wool challis. The fabrics I used were lightweight, so in one, a 12" (30.5 cm) strip reduced to 2" (5.1 cm), and in the other, a 12" (30.5 cm) strip reduced to 3" (7.6 cm). I used these to fill in around the bias-shirred sections and the small coils. It is hard to say how many are needed, but I found working with many short chenille strips easier than with longer strips, especially as the spaces to fill in became smaller and fewer.

Chenille strips: finished, raw strips, and being formed

Attach the green strips to the red felt, tucking them around the coils and bias strips. Do not fill in too tightly or the wreath will not lie flat.

Short chenille strips—some have been attached to the felt and others are ready to go.

When the chenille shirring pieces were filled in, the bias sections were too high and visually intrusive, so I trimmed them down nearly level with the chenille surface.

When the wreath was filled in, the bias strips were too high. Here, only the two on the right have been trimmed down.

Cut a length of cord or ribbon and attach it to the top of the wreath for hanging. If a backing is sewn on, attach the cord or ribbon to the felt section before sewing the backing in place.

Back of the wreath and foam core, cut slightly smaller than the felt. The foam core will hold the ornament in shape, and red cotton knit will cover the foam core and hold it in place.

Options Use ribbon for the bias-shirred sections. Add beads or metallic cording in the arrangement.

If the ornament has a tendency to bend or curve, cut a piece of foam core, plastic, or cardboard about an inch smaller than the foundation. It can be glued to the back or held in place by a layer of another fabric laid over it and sewn to the foundation. I used red knit from a repurposed t-shirt.

Back of finished wreath ornament

Pattern outline

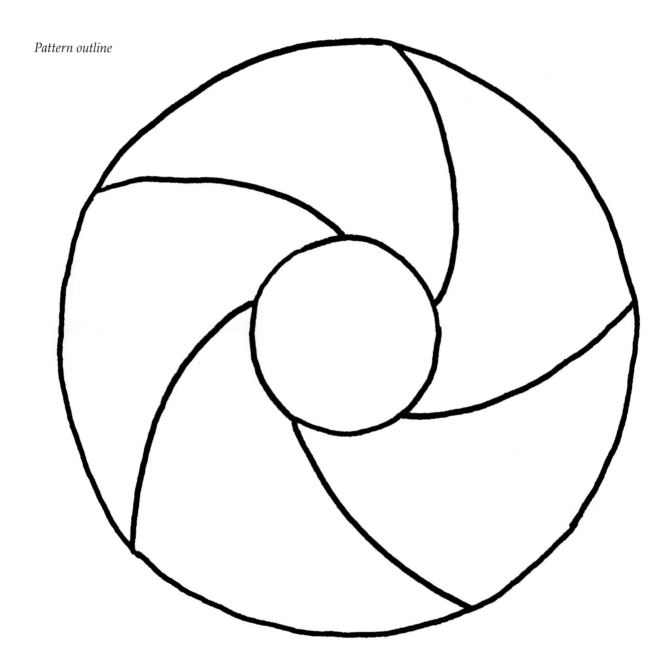

CHAPTER 5

Projects

These projects are my explorations with various materials to see how they looked in forms other than how I usually work. There are no patterns, and the directions are just a guide to how I developed them. Some I will work with again, possibly into larger pieces or as components within another work. With others, however, this time was enough . . . though I did learn something from all of them and that knowledge can be transferred to other works.

Jewelry

Some of these techniques are adaptable to making jewelry. The following projects are a wonderful way to spotlight unusual fabrics that may get overlooked in a larger project, or consider them a way to use small amounts of special fabrics and trim. Shown here are bias-shirred necklaces and coiled brooches. They are quick, versatile, fun, individualized, and easy to make. Both techniques can be used in more variations than shown here and in other forms of jewelry.

COILED NECKLACES

Techniques
Coiling, sewing

Supplies
Scissors or rotary cutter
Thread
Fabric—as shown, vintage silk ribbon and
   silk fabric
Cord or narrow ribbon
Beads—optional

Red Ribbon Necklace

ABOVE: *Bias-cut ribbon strips, rolled coils of ribbon and fabric, and uncut ribbon ready to be cut with the rotary cutter*

LEFT: *Along with the double-sided ribbon, I interspersed a few rolled strips of gold silk left over from another project.*

Finished length: 24¹/₂" (62.2 cm)

This necklace is made with a vintage silk double-sided ribbon about 4¹/₂" (11.4 cm) wide. You need a wide ribbon, or the coils will not have enough rolled layers to give structure to the coiled bead and will be difficult to handle. Each strip was cut on a 45-degree angle, about ³/₄" (1.9 cm) wide.

The ribbon has selvages, which become the ends of the strips. As it is cut on the bias, it will not unravel.

Each strip is rolled (I alternated which side was out to take advantage of the two colors), keeping the edges fairly even. Each "bead" is strung on a double thickness of heavy-duty thread as soon as it is rolled. There is no need to stitch or glue the coils before stringing.

It was easiest to roll the strips by folding the angled end over the strip, then folding and pinching the end to start the roll. This way the tail did not get in the way or stick out too much.

The outside tails add another bit of interest. If they are cut, the ribbon may start to unravel. If you do not want to see the tails, fold the end in before the last wrap around and insert the needle near the closing fold.

I used 83 beads and an 8" (20.3 cm) length of cord, doubled, for the back of the necklace. As the coils are soft, I expect with time they will settle and some of the stringing thread may show where it joins the cord. To help head this off, I snugged them up fairly close without crushing them. For this reason, it might be best to store them flat and not on a peg or hook.

When all the coils were strung, I stitched them securely to the cording on both ends. This length will allow it to slip over my head.

Black Silk and Bead Necklace

Finished length: 24" (61 cm)
This was the first beaded coil necklace I made. Using a small section of double-sided silk fabric, I cut each strip on a 45-degree angle, about $^3/_4$" (1.9 cm) wide.

Options
Make the necklace all coiled beads and longer to loop over. Make it shorter and use a clasp. Mix in several colors of ribbons or beads. Vary the width of the strips to make long and short or a graduated necklace.

The necklace features purchased beads mixed in with the black double-faced satin coiled beads.

Small coiled beads with alternating sides of the ribbon showing. If strung without purchased beads, they will tend to align tipped back and forth making a nice texture.

The fabric in various stages: uncut double-faced satin fabric, bias-cut strips, and the first few rolled sections on needle and thread

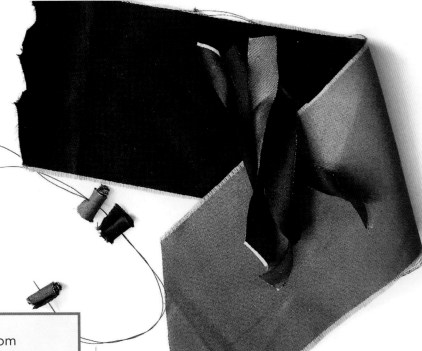

> **Tip** To help prevent the coils from flattening and the stringing thread from showing, put a knot between each coil, similar to how fine pearl necklaces are made. This knot will keep the coils from settling down on top of one another.

I was only able to get 32 coils from the fabric and filled in with various black beads; I used a thin black ribbon for the back of the necklace.

Construction and assemblage are the same as for the Red Ribbon Necklace. One caveat: Do not insert the needle too closely to the end of the rolled strip if it does not have a selvage. If the raw or cut silk edge has not been treated to stop fraying, and the end has not been folded in, it will fray and come loose.

As the length of the strip was cut on the bias, it did not unravel; however, the ends, even when cut square with the length, were soon shedding bits of thread. I did not mind the more frayed look, but the bits of fabric threads coming off were not so nice. To fix this problem, I put a non-fray solution (Fray-Chek) on each coil. Had I folded in the ends, the shedding might not have been of such concern. If using a non-fray solution, test a piece of your fabric first, as it may change the color or leave it feeling stiffer than you like.

SHIRRED NECKLACE

Techniques
Chenille shirring, sewing

Supplies
Scissors or rotary cutter
Thread
Fabric—as shown in sheer polyester chiffon
(any sheer fabric with a bit of body is best)
Cord or narrow ribbon
Fabric glue or non-fraying solution
Beads—optional

Option Use two or more layers of
fabric and gather them as
one. Use a fabric-stiffening solution on softer
fabric to help it hold its shape better.

Sheer Shirred Necklace

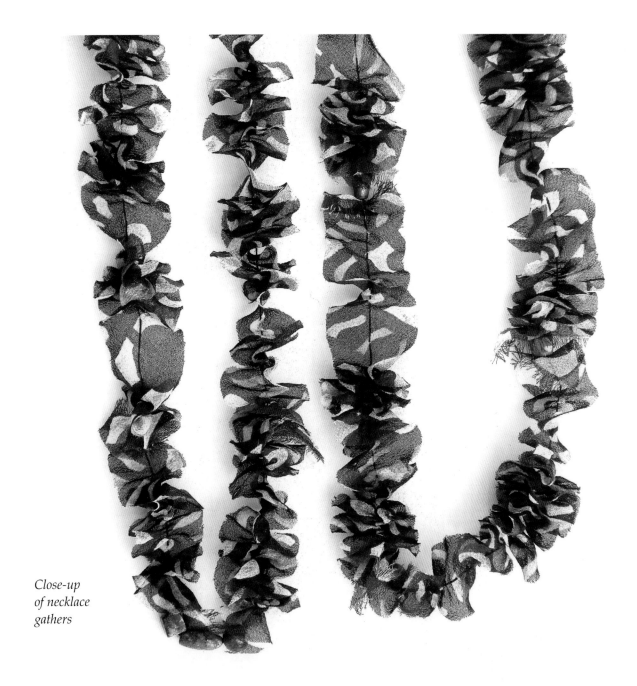

*Close-up
of necklace
gathers*

Finished length: 24" (61 cm) diameter

Cut strips of sheer fabric on the bias, $^3/_4$"–1" (1.9 cm–2.5 cm) wide. The length depends on how long you want the necklace to be and how fully it will be gathered.

Using fairly small, even stitches, make a running stitch down the center of the strip. Gather as tightly or loosely as you like. You may want to do a small backstitch at regular intervals to keep the gathers in place as gravity has a tendency to let things slide to the bottom.

Alternatively, wait until the necklace is finished, adjust the density of the gathers, then apply a drop of non-fraying solution or fabric glue to the thread at various spots to help keep them in place. Yet another option would be to string a bead, not too large or it will weigh down the fabric, at various intervals. Again, I would add a drop of non-fraying solution or fabric glue at each bead point and slide the bead against it to help hide the glue spot as well as hold the gathers in place. Be sure that the glue you use will dry clear.

Sew a ribbon to either end so it will slide over the head easily. You can make the shirring go the entire length of the necklace, but I found the gathers flattened down at the back of the neck.

Techniques

Coiling, standing wool, and sewing with beads

These brooches are best used on outerwear, hats, or totes and purses. They are not particularly resistant to abrasion, especially those made with cut strips. Torn, bias-cut strips and wool that is heavily fulled or felted would be less likely to abrade or unravel.

All of the brooches are made with strips that are $3/8"–1/2"$ (1 cm–1.3 cm) wide, and the coils are snugly wrapped; this will help maintain their shape. Wider strips with more loosely wrapped coils may work just as well—so much depends on the fabric you use. Try out different fabrics to see the effects you get.

Supplies

Scissors or cutter

Threads—heavy and lighter weight for beading

Needles—beading needle if seed beads are used; heavier, longer, and/or curved needle, as works best for you

Fabrics—as shown, these are all made with wool. Some silks may be difficult to sew through.

Pliers are optional. Sometimes it is easier to pull/push with pliers than fingers.

Pearl Brooch

The join of the center two coils is nearly invisible when the ends are nested together. The purple outside strip is sewn snugly to the inside areas between the coils, and a small loop is made at the center point of each outside coil.

Finished dimensions: 2³/₄" x 3" (7 cm x 7.6 cm)
This brooch is made using coiling and standing wool with two wool fabrics, one mottle dyed and one solid, both cut on the straight of the grain. Faux pearl beads are inserted in the outside standing wool loops.

In this design, the coils are of equal size. Using fabric of the same weight makes coiling the same size much easier. To get equal sizes you can count the rounds, cut the strips the same length, or coil them to fit a template. Slight differences will occur, but they will likely fit together smoothly.

Start with two center coils; butt the end of each coil up to the other and sew them together. This will make it look as if they were both rolled from one continuous strip to make the join smooth. Of course, rolling the coils from a continuous strip would work as well.

Join the next two coils on either side and add the others around the edge, sewing each one in as you go and facing the ends to the inside up against another coil for a neater looking finished product.

When you have a satisfactory arrangement of sewn coils, cut a long strip the same width as the coil strips. This will go around the entire piece, making loops at each coil.

Snug the end of this long strip to an inside angle where two coils meet and sew it in place. As you wrap the long strip around the outside of the coils, stitch it on the inside angles and pull in firmly to give definition to the brooch outline. At each desired point, make a small loop and test to make sure it is the right size for the beads that will be inserted. Measure and mark if needed. Stitch the base of the loop securely and sew it to the coil. If you run short of your long strip before completing the round, end it at an inside angle and start the next in the same space.

When finished, put a small drop of glue on the inside of the loops and insert the bead, being careful that any stringing holes are not exposed. You could also sew them in, taking care that stitches will not be noticeable.

Beaded Drop Brooch

Tip Hold a coil together with a straight pin until you know it is the size you want, then stitch it to keep it from coming undone.

Finished dimensions: $5^3/4" \times 3^1/4"$ (14.6 cm x 8.3 cm) This pin is made using coiling and sewing with beads. Five fabrics, cut on the straight of grain, are used to make seven coils in various sizes. Many combinations are possible, and harmony is created by repeating a couple of colors in several coils; white was used in five of the seven coils and turquoise in four.

My hand-cut strips vary a little in width, so the height of each coil may be different. Because of the varying widths, I wrapped each coil carefully to keep the edges on one side level. (It may not matter for other projects, but for this pin I wanted each coil surface to be level and smooth.) Put a straight pin in the top of the best side of the coil to help remember which side is up. If there is too much unevenness on the bottom of the coil, trim off as needed before you do any stitching.

After you've made a selection of coils, audition various arrangements on a piece of paper. Add or subtract from the coils to get the size proportions you prefer.

Once you have an arrangement that pleases you, make an outline of it so you do not lose track of your design as you sew the coils together—it happens.

Sew any two coils together, trying not to pierce the outside layer of each coil as you stitch. This way you will not have to worry about stitches making dimples on the outside of the coils.

If your coils vary in height, either from hand-cut strips or because they are made using strips of various widths, be sure to keep the bottom of the coils flat and level; this will be the back of the brooch. Any difference in coil height should be on top.

Return the two attached coils to the pattern, mark where the next coil will join in, and secure it to those already joined. Continue in this manner until all of your coils are attached to each other. Be sure to join each coil with its end facing in toward the center and, if possible, aligned with another coil's end. This will make for a smoother look and keep ends from coming loose.

Beads around the coils are added at the end with a simple running stitch. I found it easier to mark where I wanted the beads with pins to get even spacing. To

Joining Coils

How you sew coils together is not as important as making sure that the join is snug where each coil meets another. To minimize distortion when sewing, do not pierce the very outside layer of each coil. You can come through the top, being sure to reinsert the needle in the same spot it came out of, but angling it in a different direction. Pull only enough to snug up, not so much that the fabric dimples or distorts the shape. If bringing the needle through the bottom, you can insert it in another area, as the stitches will not show on the bottom. It is easier to avoid outside dimples when the coils are wrapped firmly.

fill in small gaps, I inserted a few beads and stitched them in place. Or you could glue them; be careful to assure that the bead stringing holes are not visible.

Use the stronger, heavy-weight beading thread for the beaded drop. Insert a needle through the bottom of a coil near where you want the drop to be and come out at that spot on the side of the coil, leaving a 3" (7.6 cm) tail of thread hanging at the first insertion point. Add the beads, taking care not to pull the thread tail out, ending with a small bead. Come back up through the holes of the hanging beads to the coils. Do not go back through the small bead as this will hold everything on. Make sure the small bead will not go through the bead above it. Bring the needle up near, but not in, the same hole as it was first inserted to string the beads. Firm up the beaded drop, but take care not to make them kink or allow the beading thread to show. Tie the starting and ending threads together and trim the ends.

If you wish to really tighten up the coils to each other after they are all joined, run a thread through the center of the outside coils and pull it firmly to snug them up against the inner coils.

Blue and Rust Brooch

Finished dimensions: 3" x 3" (7.6 cm x 7.6 cm)
This is another pin made using coiling and beading, but this time the fabric is cut on the bias. I used three fabrics to make five coils in two sizes. Bias strips will not unravel, but when making the coils, take care that the fabric strips are not pulled apart or stretched when wrapping, as this could distort the coils. After the coils are made, assemble as for the Beaded Drop Brooch on page 68.

The beads around the outside add interest and help hold the bias coils in shape. String about six beads, make a backstitch and come through the last bead, then string six more and repeat. This keeps the beads in alignment.

Applying the Pin Back and Backing

Place the wrong side of your assembled coils on a piece of paper and trace around the edge. Mark the inside of that tracing as the side that will go next to the bottom of the pin. It is also a good idea to place a straight pin on one side of an outside coil and a corresponding mark on the paper tracing. It is very easy to forget which side is up and exactly how it aligned on the paper pattern.

Cut out the paper pattern just slightly within the tracing line; be sure any markings are on the inside of the pattern so you can reference them. Using the pattern as a guide, cut out the fabric you will use for the brooch backing. If the fabric has a right and wrong side, be careful which side you pin the paper pattern to. Remember the wrong side of the fabric will face the backside of the brooch. Transfer the positional marking from the paper pattern to the fabric on the wrong side.

Decide how you want the pin to be positioned—which side is the top. Place the fabric backing against the back of the coils and determine where the pin back should go so that the pin will sit straight when worn. A little above the middle is good, as you don't want it flopping forward, but not too high or it will be seen.

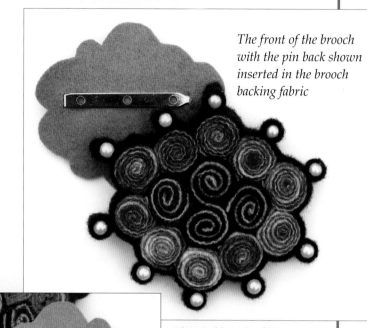

The front of the brooch with the pin back shown inserted in the brooch backing fabric

The visible side of the backing fabric with the pin back inserted and the back of the brooch to which it will be glued

Mark the ends of where the pin back will sit. Cut two small vertical slits at these markings (make them small; you can always make them larger if need be). Insert the pin back through the slits so that the business end of the pin is on the correct side of the backing fabric and the bar of the pin is on the wrong side.

If you want to "sign" your work in stitches on the backing fabric, this is the time to do it, before it is glued in place.

Apply an even layer of fabric glue to the entire back of the fabric backing and a bit under the pin bar. Press evenly and firmly to the bottom of the coils. Any glue that seeps out needs to be removed before it sets up. If the fabric backing is shy of coverage, it can usually be stretched slightly to cover the area before the glue has dried. Once the glue has dried, trim away any of the backing that is sticking out, but be very careful not to snip any of the coil fabrics.

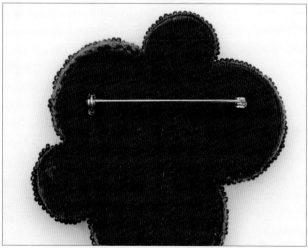

The back of the Blue and Rust Brooch with pin backing glued in place. Note the placement of the pin back on the upper half of the brooch.

Trivets

Techniques
Coiling and standing wool

Supplies
Scissors or cutter
Threads and needles—heavier, longer, and/or
    curved needle, as works best for you (Snugged)
Glue (Side by Side)
Fabrics—as shown, these are made with wool.
Pliers are optional. Sometimes it is easier to pull/
    push with pliers than fingers.

Snugged Trivet

Finished dimensions: 5" x 5^1/$_2$" (12.6 cm x 14 cm) For this little trivet, I used wool fabric samples that were rather small, 4^1/$_2$" x 2" (11.4 cm x 5.1 cm), and not suitable for hooking. I cut them into strips approximately ^{1}/$_2$" (1.3 cm) wide. Making random strip selections, I wrapped four strips to make each coil, one after another or two wrapped together.

Select coils that look good together and make an arrangement. In this case, the sizes of the coils varied slightly, as not all the wool samples were of the same weight. They will often fill in as they are snugged up to each other when you sew them together. In my first arrangement, the coils in the middle were a bit larger than the ones on the outside. There would be gaps around the outside row if I used this arrangement, so I placed the smaller coils in the center and the larger on the outside to help alleviate this.

Uncut fabric samples, rolled coils, and cut strips

In my first arrangement, the coils in the middle were larger than those on the outside, creating gaps.

Start sewing two coils together in the center and adding others around them, nestling them into the spaces between. Do not worry about stitches on the outside coils showing, since they will be covered by the next row of coils. Only on the very outside round of coils is it necessary to hide the stitches.

Stitching the center coils together

Even with this arrangement a few gaps still remained, so I wrapped a strip of black around some to expand them a bit, allowing the coils to snug up more easily. The entire trivet was also wrapped in a black strip to give it a more cohesive finished look. The black strip was secured at the inner angle of the coils where they join each other. The outside strip also covered any dimples that formed when the coils were sewn together.

Wrapping black around some of the center coils helps to fill in potential gaps. The stitches holding the black strip to the coils will be covered by the next row of coils.

To keep the stitches from showing, attach the black outside strip at the inside angle between two coils all the way around.

The bottom can be left uncovered or covered with suitable fabric, either sewn or glued on.

Assembled center coils

Side by Side Trivet

Finished dimensions: $4^1/4"$ x $5^1/4"$
(10.6 cm x 13.25 cm)

This trivet is made with fulled wool. Though not very thick, it is very dense and therefore hard to pierce with a needle or pin. The strips were hand cut about $3/8"$ (1.9 cm). For this trivet, it is important that the coils are the same size or the trivet will be asymmetrical. Make your color choices and coil as desired. After you have made your arrangement, take two coils next to each other and, with ends meeting, glue or stitch them securely. Continue in this manner until you have every coil coupled up.

> **Tip**
> If you add the small coils after the larger coils have been joined and will be gluing them, be sure to place small dots of glue on the inside of where they are to go. DO NOT put the glue on the small coils—it will get pushed up over the top as you insert them.

Cut strips for the outer border.

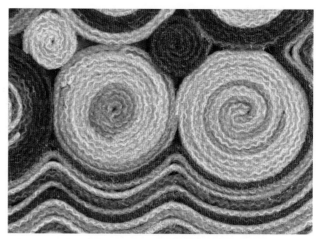

Close-up of the large coils, small fill-in coils, and the layered border. Be sure to push the felt strip well into each angle between the coils, or the outline will lose its wavy shape.

TOP: To give a smoother finish, the coils have been glued together in pairs with the ends nested together.
ABOVE: All the coils are glued together before wrapping the outer layers.

Start gluing or sewing the paired-up coils until your piece is solid. The holes between the four coils may be filled with small coils if you wish. These small coils may be added as you go or at the end.

Leave the edge as is or wrap with one or more layers of wool, beginning and ending the outside layers at an inside angle between two coils. Be sure, if gluing, that you really press into the angle between coils as you go around.

When finished, glue or sew a bottom of suitable fabric on the trivet. This will help it stay together, as the glue is not as durable as stitches would be.

Fiber Art

Fiber art is becoming more accepted into the realm of general art and fine craft. Previously, most pieces made of fiber, such as quilts, rugs, and clothing, were exclusively for a practical purpose and relegated in the scope of women's domestic sphere. Not to say that esthetic appeal was unimportant—quite the contrary. But the primary purpose was utilitarian.

Now rugs and quilts are not just taken from the floor and bed to hang on the wall, they are made specifically for artistic display and, in the case of installation pieces, for much larger spaces indoors and out. Not everyone has the space to devote a wall or room to a piece of art, so small fiber pieces are perfect solutions. These smaller pieces are also a good way to experiment with techniques before committing to something larger or as an end in themselves.

One of the aspects to make an artwork more important and "artful" is how it is mounted, framed and presented. Though it is beyond the scope of this book, I highly encourage anyone creating pieces intended for a wall, table, easel, and so on to consider how it will be displayed. By presenting your work with considered thought, you advance the appreciation of fiber in the art world.

Denim DNA

Finished dimensions: 12¹/₂" x 12¹/₂"
(31.5 cm x 31.5 cm)

Technique
Coiling

Supplies
Scissors—though strips are all torn for this project, you will need them
Thread
Needles
Pins
Fabric glue
Stretcher frame
Foam core
Stapler and staples
Fabrics—various denims and shirt-weight linen
Pliers are optional. Sometimes it is easier to pull/push with pliers than fingers.

What to do with your old blue jeans and workshirts? They are not always easy to sew, but they tear into very useable strips with soft edges and lovely colors. Denim is woven with different colored weft and warp threads; this means there will be different edge colors depending on which way it is torn. Tear in both directions to make the most of the denim coloration, or in one direction if you prefer just one color. Tear strips from ¹/₂"–³/₄" (1.3 cm–1.9 cm) wide. Coil the strips, blending or alternating colors as you wish.

Caution
When pushing/pulling the needle through a coil from back to front, be very careful that you do not inadvertently cause the core of the coil to be pushed/pulled out. The center of the coil is held in by pressure alone and can easily be pushed/pulled out and unwind. If this happens it is very difficult to coil it back up and reinsert it. I know this from experience.

To prevent this, press down on the center of the coil as the needle is pulled up through it. After the thread is pulled up through the coil, reinsert the needle at a slight angle to go down through to the back.

Side view of the coils

The edge of the frame with denim strips affixed. BELOW: Rug binding tape is glued on over the stapled edge as a finishing touch. Notice that the stitches that attach the coils to the front show on the back of the foam core.

Sewing through many layers of denim can be a near impossibility, so use fabric glue to secure the ends of the coils. Arrange the coils as you wish; when satisfied, use small dabs of glue to hold the coils to each other, being careful that the glue is used only where it will secure the coils and will not be seen.

Normally I would attach the coils to the foundation fabric and then mount the entire piece, but I reversed it for this project. I mounted the foundation fabric on the frame and then attached the coils.

Make a stretcher frame (be sure it is square), glue a piece of foam core cut to size on the top of the frame, and weight it down with books until dry to prevent warping. Wrap and staple the foundation fabric around the frame, folding in the corners tightly.

Position the coils on the mounted foundation fabric, using long pins to anchor them into the foam core. Now start to stitch the coils onto the foundation fabric through the foam core. (If you only attach them to the foundation fabric, they might tip over a bit; this way they will stay upright.) Start with the knot on the top side, hidden within a coil; if you start on the foam core side, the knot might pull through the foam core and loosen the attachment.

Note The screw eyes and wire are affixed to the inside of the frame, not the back of it. This is a safety measure to help prevent the screw eyes and wire from catching on any work it is put against or scratching walls or other surfaces. It is easier to put the screw eyes in before the foam core is glued to the front of the frame—I have yet to remember to do that.

I did not sew through every coil, but tried to catch an edge of as many as reasonable. They are glued together and one hopes that that will hold them securely. However, glue dries out in time, and the bonds may not be as secure as one would like to think.

Strips torn to 1" (2.5 cm) wide form the edging along the outside of the frame. Apply a bead of glue the length of each strip, spread it evenly, and affix strips to the edge of the frame in as many layers as you wish—I used six. Be careful that no glue soaks through the last strip, as it will be visible when dry.

Glue on rug binding tape to make a nice clean look on the back and prevent scratching any surface it comes in contact with. Add screw eyes and wire if you plan to hang the piece.

Trail Map
(Polar Fleece and Glue)

Finished dimensions: 22" x 26" (55.9 cm x 66 cm) at widest points

Techniques
Standing wool (or in this case standing polar fleece) and coiling

Supplies
Scissors
Glue that is suitable for the fabric used
Pins—long pins with colored heads are best
Fabrics—as shown, various types of polar fleece
Pliers are optional. Sometimes it is easier to pull/ push with pliers than fingers.
Styrofoam or foam rubber surface
Weights to hold glued strips and shapes to form; I used hardcover books.

Gluing a strip folded lengthwise

Strips of polar fleece used showing both front and back:

Navy with leaves—*lengthwise cut, 42" (106.7 cm), rough texture (not reversible), medium stretch in both directions, thick*

Stripe—*lengthwise cut, 54" (137.2 cm), smooth both sides, lengthwise stretch is minimal, lots of stretch crosswise, thinnest*

Orange—*crosscut, 49" (124.5 cm), smooth both sides, minimal stretch lengthwise, good stretch crosswise, medium weight*

Purple plaid—*crosscut, 51" (129.5 cm), rough one side, slightly smoother other side, heavy stretch crosswise, nearly no stretch lengthwise, thick*

Dark gray with white tips—*crosscut, 55" (139.7 cm), very rough (not reversible), more stretch crosswise than lengthwise, thickest*

Lime green—*crosscut, 62" (157.5 cm), smooth one side, rough one side, stretch is minimal in both directions, medium thick*

Green/white plaid—*crosscut, 51" (129.5 cm), rough texture (not reversible), stretchy in both directions, thick*

Darkest plaid—*crosscut, 42" (106.7 cm), slightly rough on both sides, minimal stretch in either direction, medium weight*

I decided to try a piece using Polar fleece. Rather than sewing I used glue, but I could not use hot glue, which would melt the fleece. An entire 8-ounce bottle of Aleene's Quick Dry Tacky Glue was needed for this piece. It dries clear and flexible, though flexible does not mean soft, and once the strip is glued, the stretch is gone.

There is a lot of variety in fleeces. Some fleece has a stretchy direction and a not-so-stretchy direction, some are stretchy in both directions, some are reversible, and others have a right and wrong side. They also come in a wide range of thicknesses, from very thin to quite thick. I used a variety of fleeces and cut the strips both crosswise and lengthwise. They are described with their color above from left to right.

To prepare the strips, cut fleece in 2" (5.1 cm) wide strips, fold them in half lengthwise, and glue the smoother side of the fleece together the length of the strip. (Thicker fleece needed weights to hold the strips together until the glue dried, so I stacked books on them.) One could also try skipping this step and using the fleece in single layers.

Glue two prepared strips together by running a bead of glue on one strip only and start to shape them into your design. When coiling two strips together, or wrapping multiple strips back upon themselves, you need to put glue on both sides of the strips or only one will be glued. Be careful not to put glue on the side that will be your final outside edge. For example, in this piece, the glue would need to be applied to both sides of the dark-grey strip but not on the outside of the lime-green strip (if that was to be the final outside edge). It will be obvious if you missed an area; you can glue those areas as you find them or at the end when you check the project over.

The center of any two-toned coil looks better when one end is wrapped over the other end to start.

Note Using hot glue will make your project proceed much faster, as the glue sets up very quickly. However, use hot glue only on natural fibers, not on polyester, nylon, or other synthetic fibers that may melt. Check first to see how the glue will affect your fabric.

Pin the strips to each other and to a large sheet of Styrofoam or foam rubber (that the glue will not hurt) to hold the shape until the glue dries. Use long pins with colored heads or you risk losing them in the fleece. Work quickly, as the glue drips and you don't want to glue the fleece to the working surface.

Strips are folded, wrapped, coiled, and glued as the free-form design grows.

I used books to help hold the glued strips in shape until they dried, although something like a large cribbage board with lots of holes and pegs would have been a better idea. Work in sections and do not try to assemble too big a section at once.

Books or similar objects can be used as braces to keep the strips in place until the glue dries.

After the section is dry, be sure to remove pins before starting the next section or you will have a very hard time finding them. I needed pliers to remove some of the pins that had been inserted into a glue area.

Gaps are likely to happen, even when the fabric is pinned and pressed together, especially at tight turns and angles. They can be left as part of the design or filled in with shorter sections or coiled pieces.

When inserting a smaller piece into a hole or gap, glue the small piece to itself, then line the opening it is going into with glue. Do not put the glue on the piece being inserted. This prevents glue getting pushed up over the top.

You may need to run a few internal stitches or add more glue to secure loose places after you are done.

LEFT: *Pins held the pieces in place until the glue dried. Using pins with colored heads makes it easier to find and remove them.*

Gaps may show up, especially at tight angles.

LEFT: *Gaps and empty spots can be filled in with small coils. For more interest, use a contrasting color, or use matching fleece to provide continuity.*

Maze

Finished dimensions: 12¹/₄" x 15" (31.1 cm x 38.1 cm) at widest points

Techniques
Standing wool, coiling

Supplies
Scissors and/or rotary cutter
Braid maker

Iron
Thread
Needles—heavier, longer, and/or curved needle, as works best for you
Pins
Fabrics—as shown, this is made with shirt- and skirt-weight wool
Pliers are optional. Sometimes it is easier to pull/ push with pliers than fingers.

I used shirt- and skirt-weight wools for this project; some tended to unravel easily, so I decided to have no exposed raw edges, except for individual coils. I cut strips 2" (5.1 cm) wide and put the strips through a braid maker for braided rugs. This folded the edges in to the middle and I pressed the folds as I pulled the braid maker along the strip. I folded the sides together and stitched them closed, which gave me a $^1/_2$" (1.3 cm) strip with no raw edges. The ends of the strips were tucked in and stitched closed.

With the seam side down, I started coiling, folding, and arranging the strips spontaneously, pinning the coils and folds as I went. When one strip ended, I joined in another until all the strips were pinned in place—to each other. I used no foundation support for this project.

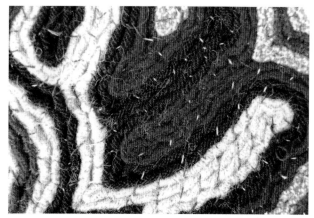

White stitches seam each strip closed; dark stitches hold each side of the strip to the next one.

Before sewing, pins held the free-form design together. With no foundation fabric below it, the floor can be seen between some of the spaces.

I flipped the piece over and started sewing the strips together, sewing one side of a strip to the one next to it. How tightly to pull the stitches is a test-and-see method—too tightly and the piece may distort, too loosely and it will be sloppy looking and weaker. With coils or complicated intersections I ran a few interior stitches to keep the piece in shape. As the piece was held together with only straight pins, I found it necessary to place it on a flat surface while sewing. Picking it up caused pins to pull out and the piece was in jeopardy of falling apart. This sewing part was the most time-consuming aspect and took far longer than I would have thought.

Sewing changed the dimensions and proportions of the piece as it drew tighter together. (At times it seemed a third hand would have been convenient!) If I had done a specific design in the center, such as an animal outline, I would have sewn that together first to maintain its shape and then added the outer coils. It may have been easier to sew the strips together as I went along, however the spontaneity of the design might have been lost.

As I sewed the strips to each other, gaps appeared as areas were pulled together or apart; these were perfect places to insert coiled strips, some cut on the bias and others torn or cut on the straight. Liking the look of the inserted coils, I decided to surround nearly the entire piece with them—a nice thing about this technique is that you can keep adding on as you go.

The coils were sewn with an interior thread making an X through the middle, and then arranged around the perimeter. Each one was sewn to the strips and the coil next to it. (Generally I do not want stitches on the coils to show, but as I wanted the entire piece to be outlined with a black strip, I did not have to be as concerned with that.)

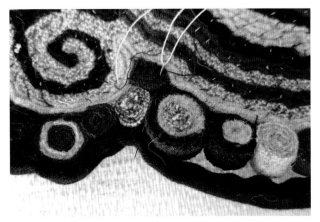

Working from the back, sew the outside strip to the inside angle between the coils to make a smoother edge.

Do not cut the outside strip length until the piece is completely sewn. Stitch the outside strip only to the spaces between the coils; this will look smoother and will snug the outside strip tight to the piece and prevent gaps. If you need to end a strip and start another, do it at the angle between two coils, where it will be less noticeable.

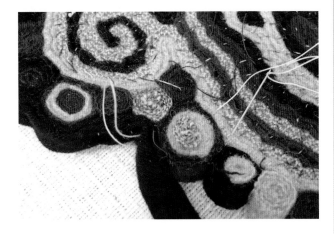

To get a good secure stitch, run the needle well into the design, not just into the outside coil.

Sew in at angles to get a good secure stitch. Run the needle well into the design, not just into the outside coil, to get a good grip and not risk them pulling out.

White thread (used for example only) shows where the outside strip is attached to the body of the piece.

Along the edge, white stitches show where the outside strip is attached to the body of the piece.

The benefit of sewing it as I did (after assembling the design) meant that all the stitches were on the bottom, and the top has a nicely rounded and undistorted look.

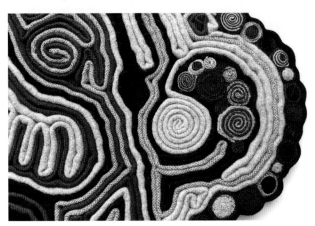

Detail of the finished piece

However, if the fabric had been very thick and was sewn tightly on the bottom, the piece would begin to hump as the bottom became tighter than the top. (Though with thicker fabric there may have been no need to seam the strips closed together before wrapping the strips into a design—that would have been the standard standing wool technique.)

If the strips were sewn together as the design is being developed, the stitches could come out the side and the next strip would cover any stitches that might show.

This method would be great for a mola-inspired design, or as an abstract floral or animal pattern. (Molas are hand-stitched reverse-appliqué fabric art made by the Kuna people on the San Blas Islands off the coast of Panama.)

Barrier

Finished dimensions: 16" x 15 $^1/_2$" (40.6 cm x 39.4 cm)

Finding three damaged 100% cashmere sweaters at a yard sale for one dollar each was too good to pass up and provided me with the inspiration to make a coiled piece from cut sweaters. Gathering other damaged sweaters of cashmere, merino, Shetland (turquoise), and acrylic (oh horrors!—but the pea green color worked well with the others), along with a dark multicolored sweater from a thrift store (that had shrunk madly and densely after a machine washing), I cut the sweaters crosswise into $^1/_2$"–1" (1.3 cm–2.5 cm) strips. Cutting sweater strips lengthwise makes a firmer coil.

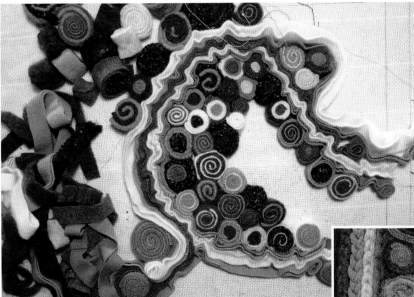

The components: cut strips and coils, with the shirred strips attached. This was the auditioning stage, and the inner coils were not yet sewn in.

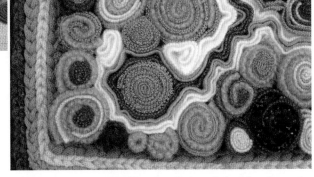

Detail of a corner showing the chain-stitched border and close-up of coils.

After making many coils, I needed a "structure" to lay them out against. I created several layers of shirring in a free-form design and stitched the shirred strips to monk's cloth, ending each shirred strip in a coil. Next, I auditioned the coils in various combinations and decided to use the smaller and shorter coils inside the shirred barrier and the larger and taller coils outside.

Once the inner coils were sewn in place, I chain stitched the border with four rows of $1/4"$ (.6 cm) strips, most cut out of the sweaters lengthwise (they stretch less this way than if cut crosswise). This chain stitching needs to be done loosely, or the foundation will pull in and distort the whole piece. Even if you are working on a frame, the tension of the chain stitching will pull the foundation in once it is off the frame. It is a good idea to remove the piece from the frame as you go to make sure the chain stitching is not too tight. Check it often at first until you know how loosely you need to work.

Chain stitching is a crochet stitch (use your rug hook) where a loop is drawn up through the foundation, but the loop stays on the hook as the hook is inserted back through the foundation. The strip on the bottom is hooked, and another loop is drawn up through the foundation and pulled through the loop still on the hook from the previous stitch. This is done around the border. The end of a strip is pulled up through the last loop and then pulled through the foundation to the back to anchor the last loop. The first loop of the next strip is pulled up in the last loop and the process is repeated. This leaves short ends on the back.

With the chain stitching in place, I added the rest of the coils, making small ones to fill in gaps. Since many of the gaps were too small for coils but large enough to show the foundation, I used a color that matched the inner row of chain stitching to hook along the edge between the coils and chain stitching and fill in these areas.

I used strips from one of the sweaters for the binding, which I sewed very closely to the last row of chain stitching and folded to the back.

CHAPTER 6

Gallery of Fiber Artists

Through workshops, exhibits, word of mouth, and the Internet, examples of remarkable and varied works of standing wool and coiling have caused quite a bit of excitement in the fiber art world. The early American hand-sewn rug-making techniques of shirring are also being revived and finding new expressions.

Fiber art is becoming appreciated in a growing market and ever more popular at all levels—even garnering exhibits in museums and high-end galleries. For example, the Parrish Art Museum, in Southampton, New York, exhibited Mary Queen of the Universe from October 25, 2014 through January 20, 2015, showcasing the "scrolled" works of Stephen and William Ladd. Their pieces were made from sections of rolled cotton belt webbing they had purchased from a factory going out of business.

I asked an array of artists and makers if I might showcase their work in a gallery section of this book. Here I have curated a selection of the fiber works they offered using shirring and standing wool

techniques and other related forms, some of which defy classification. They show how versatile and exciting these techniques can be. The examples shown range from simple, folksy, and charming to amazing pieces of installation art—all take the simple means of folding and sewing fabric to new and thrilling arenas.

I have included the comments of the artists, edited only for clarity. Many have offered insights into their inspirations and explanations on how they did their work. Some of the descriptions and terms used may not be how I have defined them; it is up to the artist and maker to label her work, which demonstrates that it is not about the label, but the effect that counts. All works are designed and made by the artist unless otherwise noted.

I give enormous thanks to all for sharing their work and expanding the exploration and appreciation of how these techniques are used.

Please remember that these pieces are under the copyright of each artist and may not be replicated without her express permission.

Ali Strebel

Dayton, Ohio, U.S.; www.alistrebeldesigns.com

Ali Strebel started her fiber business and has worked in design since 1986. She is self-taught, inspired by antique rugs, and discovered some of the shirring techniques in *American Sewn Rugs*.

Dark Bloom,
22" x 28" (55.9 cm x 71.1 cm),
January 2014

Rug hooking, appliqué, standing wool, pleat shirring, bias shirring, chenille shirring, and hand-stitched embroidery with hand-dyed wool, antique wool blankets, old lace, and buttons.

Ali designed and made this piece as a teaching guide for a workshop.

ANNIE MOLNER

Detail of
Dark Bloom

Standing Wool Geometric, *18¹/₂" x 25" (47 cm x 63.5 cm)*
Designed by Ali Strebel and Jenny Rupp and created by Ali Strebel, April 2015

Rug hooking, standing wool, needle felting, and couching with wool, wool roving, and yarn.

This piece was designed as a challenge in combining different techniques to achieve an interesting work. The fibers were hand dyed.

Heart Filled,
18" x 18" (45.7 cm x 45.7 cm),
January 2014

Hooking, felting, standing wool, and bias shirring with wool, wool roving, and rayon ribbon.

Ali designed and made *Heart Filled* as a teaching tool to encourage students to try something new.

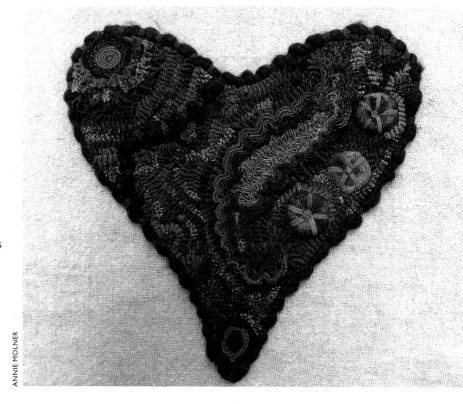

Alice Rudell

New York, New York, U.S.
    Alice learned rug hooking from Marilyn Bottjer in 1992 and shirring in 2010 from observing antique rugs.

TRACY JAMAR

Shirred Flowers,
20" x 20" (50.8 cm x 50.8 cm),
2015

Hooking, shirring, appliqué, and beading with wool, cotton, polyester, linen, silk, plastic beads, netting, and cotton lace on linen.
    This colorful piece was inspired by Alice's garden in upstate New York.

Detail of
Shirred Flowers

House of Gold,
31" x 31" (78.7 cm x 78.7 cm),
2011

Hooking, shirring, and raveling with wool, polyester, silk, netting, and brin on linen.

Alice's inspiration for *House of Gold* was "the intense glare of the setting sun on a neighbor's house, melting it into the glittering field and sparkling lake."

CLIFF GARDINER

Homage to Hooking and Shirring,
32" x 30" (81.3 cm x 76.2 cm),
2010

Hooking and shirring with wool and silk on linen.

Alice's garden was again the inspiration for her work, this time seen through the window at dusk.

BRAD STANTON

CLIFF GARDINER

Yesteryear,
29" x 28" (73.7 cm x 71.1 cm),
2013

Hooking, shirring, appliqué, and braiding with wool, silk, polyester, lace, netting, brin, cotton, linen, raffia, and mallard feathers on linen.

 "A pile of fancy fabrics, my disintegrating wedding dress, and a lawn full of ducks" was the inspiration for this piece, according to Alice.

Detail of
Yesteryear

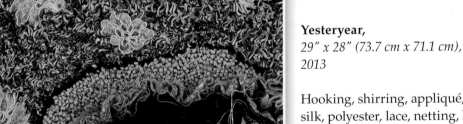

Betsy Reed

Claverack, New York, U.S.; www.heavens-to-betsy.com

Betsy learned the techniques from Carol Weatherman and *American Sewn Rugs.* She owns Heavens to Betsy, which sells supplies for hooking, standing wool, and other fiber needs.

BETSY REED

Lollipop Flower Basket, *24" x 36" (61 cm x 91.4 cm), May 2015*

Hooking and standing wool on linen. The wool for the hooked strips was torn, and $1/2$" (1.3 cm) strips were used for the standing wool.

Betsy adapted this design from an antique rug.

Carol Weatherman

Mustang, Oklahoma, U.S.; www.thesampling.net

Carol has been rug hooking since 1988 and using the technique of coiling since 2012. She is primarily self-taught. She teaches coiling and always provides a packet with curved, long, and chenille needles to her students, as they are each useful at various tasks. "Once you are shown the techniques and the supplies are on hand, it really is exciting and easy to do. Just by adding standing wool to some of the elements and then finishing with regular hooking will make it unusual. In the end you have created a wonderful piece of art."

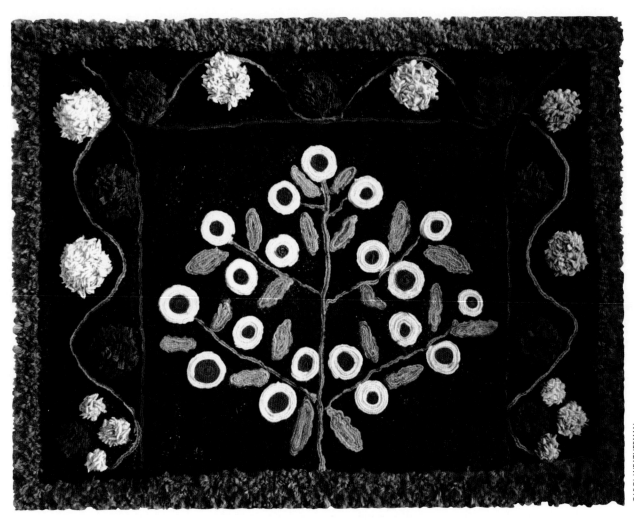

1871, *19" x 25" (48.3 cm x 63.5 cm), 2015*

Coiling, hooking, and puffing (see explanation below) with wool and wool yarn on linen.

This piece was inspired by elements in a vintage rug. The border is hooked with three shades of yarn, with every fifth loop clipped to replicate the look on the inspiration rug. "In the antique rug there appeared to be puffballs in the corners. I hooked strips high and low and then clipped each loop, but also [formed] the hooking into a circular shape."

Fire Wheel,
15" x 18" (38.1 cm x 45.7 cm),
2015

Coiling and hooking with wool on linen.

The inspiration for this piece was a wildflower watercolor. Although it came out quite differently than the inspiration, Carol is pleased with the shapes. A friend suggested the name *Fire Wheel*, as this is the name the Native Americans call these flowers; she knows them as Indian paintbrushes. These flowers are wild in her area and quite brilliantly colored. Although Carol is more subdued in her color palette, she loves the effect of the bright wool when used on edge in the standing wool coils.

CAROL WEATHERMAN

Standing Wool Floral,
22" x 17" (55.9 cm x 43.2 cm),
2013

Coiling and hooking with wool on linen.

An early hooked rug pattern was the inspiration for this piece.

CAROL WEATHERMAN

Gail Becker

Turlock, California, U.S.; www.gailbeckerrughooking.com

Gail has been rug hooking since 1999. She has been using the standing wool technique since 2008, having learned it from Diana Blake Gray's book, *Traditional Shirred and Standing Wool Rugs*.

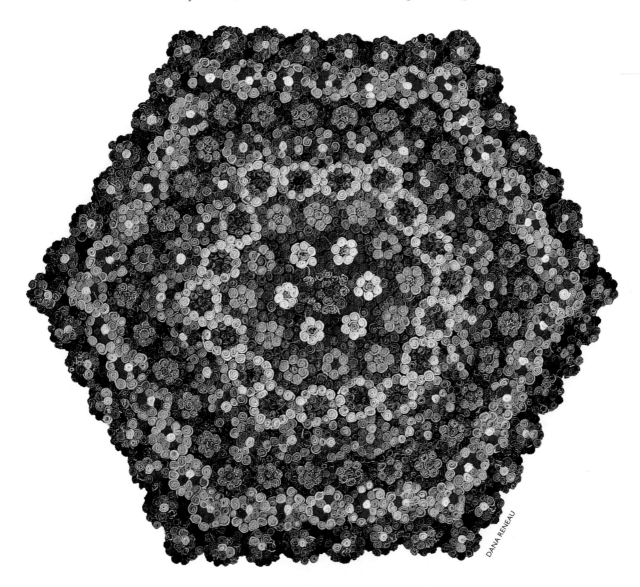

Beaded Garden, *13" (33 cm) diameter hexagon x ³/₄" (1.9 cm), May 2015*

Beaded standing wool, sewn in rounds with DMC Baroque cotton thread.

Gail's husband collects paperweights, and millefiori designs are a particular favorite. The beaded standing wool rugs resemble that type of paperweight and are even referred to as millefiori beaded rugs by Diana Blake Gray.

Gill Curwen

Great Orton, Carlisle, Cumbria, England; www.bappleandjojo.weebly.com; www.facebook.com/bappleandjojo
   Gill taught herself the standing wool technique from a Diana Blake Gray book. She has been making rag rugs since 1995 and working with standing wool since 2009 after completing a bachelor of arts in floorcovering design.

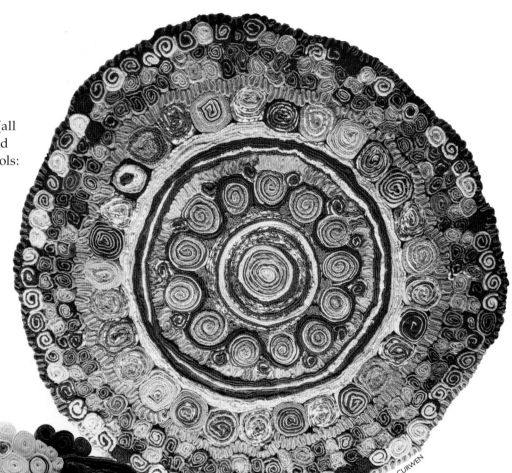

GILL CURWEN

Cartwheel,
48" (121.9 cm) diameter,
May 2013

Traditional standing wool (all sewn with linen thread) and shirring using recycled wools: sweaters, skirts, scarves, blankets, hats, socks, and coats—all at least 80% wool.
   Millefiori work and stained glass windows were the inspirations for this design.

GILL CURWEN

Quillie Ram,
48" x 30" x 1" (121.9 cm x 76.2 cm x 2.5 cm),
February 2015

Traditional standing wool (all sewn with linen thread), or quillies, and braiding using local Cumbrian and United Kingdom wools: Herdwick, Shetland, Ryeland, and recycled lamb's wool blankets.
   The members of The Wool Clip Cooperative were asked to produce pieces using Herdwick wool to complement the accompanying photo exhibition, Herdwick—A Portrait of Lakeland by Ian Lawson.

Sunburst, *72" x 36" x 1"*
(182.9 cm x 91.4 cm x 2.5 cm),
February 2014

Traditional standing wool (all sewn with linen thread), free-form standing wool, and shirring using recycled fabrics—sweaters, skirts, scarves, blankets, hats, socks, and coats—all at least 80% wool. Select wools were hand dyed.

   Gill was inspired by a local sunset and the fiery colors in the wools she used for this piece.

GILL CURWEN

Sunburst
in progress

Jan Whitlock

Miller Place, New York, U.S.; www.janwhitlockinteriors.com

Jan is a strong proponent of creating your own unique works and not copying the designs of antique rugs, even if they are in the public domain. Obviously, she says, be inspired by elements in those rugs, but alter them: play with scale, combine elements from several objects (not just other textiles), repeat elements, arrange them differently, use and combine various techniques, etc.

Jan has been in the fiber field for years, has worked in textile design and marketing, became an antiques dealer in 1999, and is well known and respected for her early antique textiles. Jan and I worked on a book about early American rugs, *American Sewn Rugs: Their History with Exceptional Examples.* Because of that book she decided to try her hand at some of the techniques and has been using them to create rugs only since 2012.

TRACY JAMAR

Cat with Fern Fronds,
31" x 39" (78.7 cm x 99.1 cm), 2015

Bias, chenille, and bundled shirring, appliqué, sewn yarn, embroidery, and braiding with wool, antique paisley, cotton, yarns, and buttons.

Jan made this work to teach herself the various techniques inspired by the antique rugs found while doing research for *American Sewn Rugs: Their History with Exceptional Examples.*

Detail of
Cat with Fern Fronds

Horses and Flowers, *20" x 29" (50.8 cm x 73.7 cm), 2015*

TRACY JAMAR

Straight and bias shirring with wool fabric, wool twill tape, and leather.

The image for the horses comes from a quilt top seen in preview for a Sotheby's auction. The center floral pot was inspired from an antique shirred rug in *American Sewn Rugs.*

Jan started without a frame and did most of the design that way. Eventually, she acquired a frame and found it was much easier and faster with a frame. She prefers the look of the lighter weight wools, but found it takes twice as long, if not more.

She "cheated" on the background and bought wool twill tape so she "wouldn't have to cut a gazillion strips." Liking the end result, she would do it that way again. She experimented with silk grosgrain ribbon to expand her color palette with hopes of not needing to buy or find so many different wool colors, but found it was hard to work with. She did find a man's sport jacket in lamb's wool at the thrift store; it provided plenty of usable fabric and was a pleasure to sew.

Jan found that if she gathered the shirring strips into heavier ripples, the effect was not what she wanted; it was better when the waviness happened naturally.

Jane Jackson

Alnwick, Northumberland, England; www.brightseedtextiles.com

Jane has been working with fibers since 2005.

"I was taught how to rag rug by Margaret Kenny, a fellow textile artist, at an adult education class." Jane always works with Harris Tweed, "which I love because of its unique historical heritage, its rough texture, and the wide range of colors and patterns. Harris Tweed is the only fabric in the world to be governed by its own Act of Parliament, which states that by law it must be hand-woven by islanders at their homes in the remote Scottish Islands of the Outer Hebrides. Harris Tweed first became fashionable in the nineteenth century when it was worn by British royalty and aristocracy to go shooting. Because of its origin as a fabric to be worn outdoors, it is traditionally associated with drab brown and green colors. But due to the increasing demand from the world of fashion, it is now available in a fantastic range of bright colors, which suits me well as I just love color."

Evening Blue II,
26" x 11" x 1¹/₄"
(66 cm x 28 cm x 3 cm),
February 2015

Prodding and standing wool with Harris Tweed (hand-woven from 100% pure new wool).

According to Jane, this piece and its companion *Crimson*, below, were "inspired by paintings by Bernat Klein, who was a textile designer, artist, and colorist."

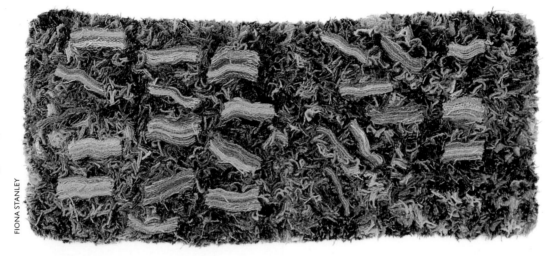

FIONA STANLEY

Crimson,
24³/₄" x 11¹/₂" x 1¹/₄"
(63 cm x 29 cm x 3 cm),
January 2015

Prodding and standing wool with Harris Tweed (hand-woven from 100% pure new wool).

"I usually use the technique of hooking to make my work, but in this case prodding seemed the best

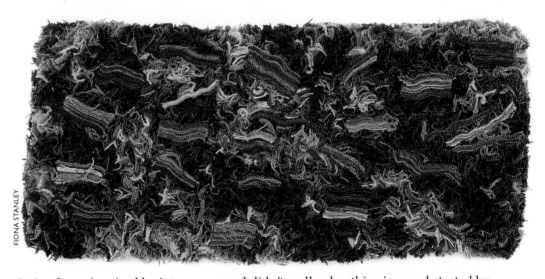

FIONA STANLEY

approach to translate the painting I was inspired by into a rag rug. I didn't really plan this piece and started by stitching the standing wool pieces of tweed into place and then prodded around them, continually referencing the painting I was working from. I packed in as much fabric as I could into the piece, as I wanted the surface to be really solid. I trimmed the surface after completion to emphasize the marbled quality of the design."

Detail of **Moss & Bark,**
24^1/$_2$" x 8" x ^{3}/$_4$"
(62 cm x 20 cm x 2 cm),
2011

Hooking, standing wool, quilling, and coiling with Harris Tweed (hand-woven from 100% pure new wool), wool yarn, and semi-precious stone beads.

"This piece is the first of a pair I made that were both inspired by some photographs I took of a gnarled old tree trunk, with very rough bark and lots of moss growing on it. This piece is slightly unusual, as my work is usually very brightly colored, but in this case I decided to use naturalistic colors."

Detail of **Purple Tree,**
36^1/$_4$" x 5" x ^{3}/$_4$"
(92 cm x 13 cm x 2 cm),
February 2011

Hooking, standing wool, quilling, and coiling with Harris Tweed (hand-woven from 100% pure new wool), wool yarn, and semi-precious stone beads.

This is the second piece inspired by a photograph of an old tree trunk. "The first piece (*Moss & Bark*) was done in naturalistic colors that emulated the actual colors of the bark and moss. I decided to make this, the second piece, in a funky color and picked purple because it is the opposite of green.

"I didn't really plan this piece and started by stitching the quilled pieces into place, followed by the coiling, and then the standing wool. I oversewed the coiling with different colored Herdwick yarns, which is very rough and hairy, to add more texture. I then hooked into the remaining areas, sewing on the semi-precious stone beads last. I trimmed the standing wool right down after completion and frayed it to reflect the rough texture of the tree bark."

JANE JACKSON

JANE JACKSON

June Myles

Redding, Connecticut, U.S.

After moving from New York City to the country, June found antiques shows to be a substitute for museums. It was at one of those shows that she came across a pair of hooked mittens that intrigued her, and when a hooking class was offered at a nearby adult education center, she became "hooked." That was in 1991 and she is still connected to some of the other participants from that class.

Shown here are two pieces from June's "Men" series. "When I hooked the first man I did not intend to create a series, but the first man was such fun—and one followed another to the point that I now live with quite a few men. None needs to be entertained, fed, have their laundry done, or will walk out! Instead, they are leaned on and walked over with nary a complaint! To dispel any thoughts to the contrary, I really like men and have lived a lot of my life largely among them—often as the sole female."

Laughter Keeps You Young
20" x 19" (50.8 cm x 48.3 cm), 2013

Hooking and shirring with hand-dyed wool.

Upon seeing the effect Alice Rudell achieved with shirring in *Yesteryear*, June was inspired to use shirring in her next man. "Looking through portraits of Elizabethan gentleman with their grand ruffs, no one spoke to me. One day there was a tiny print of George Bernard Shaw on the editorial page of the *Wall Street Journal*; his wonderfully flowing beard was just what shirring was meant to portray.

"Shirring is a pain in the neck technique, but it does make a grand beard. The full George Bernard Shaw quote is 'You don't stop laughing when you grow old, you grow old when you stop laughing,' but I would have grown old hooking all of that!"

TRACY JAMAR

TRACY JAMAR

What's Up?,
16¹/₂" x 12¹/₂" (41.2 cm x 31.8 cm), 2015

Hooking and shirring with hand-dyed wool.

This man's moustache was another opportunity to use shirring. June's collection of men now includes a chef, a fiddler, a mid-eighteenth century Persian manservant, a philosopher, a French farmer, an Afghan mullah, and a banker—"everyone except the candlestick maker." With more men to come, maybe she will hook one of them as well. Some are large and full figured, while others are the face alone. Several of her men can be seen in her books, *If Wool Could Talk— Hooked Rugs: A Memoir* and *Men Only…Mostly*.

TRACY JAMAR

Painting with Wool, *24" x 24" (61 cm x 61 cm), 2014*

Hooking and shirring with hand-dyed wool.

    Jim Dine's etching of paintbrushes and a Ralph Lauren paint ad were the inspiration for this piece. "The brushes seem destined for shirring, and it was fun 'mixing the paint' for each brush."

Kira Mead

Albany, Western Australia, AU; https://accidentalrugmaker.wordpress.com/; https://www.facebook.com/AccidentalRugmaker; https://www.facebook.com/Standingwoolrugs?fref=ts

"I learnt to crochet as a child, and to this day still love it. [I do everything] from baby blankets, free-form crochet and knitting fusion, and glass bead necklaces crocheted with fishing line. Along the way I have also indulged in embroidery and tapestry."

Kira's first exposure to standing wool was in October 2014 via a video on YouTube by Tejo Remy and René Veenhuizen called "Accidental Carpets." That inspired her to try the technique, and from then on she is self-taught. She is currently working with chain stitch hooked rugs.

Rose Gelato,
$33^1/_2$" x $29^1/_2$" x $1^1/_4$"
(85cm x 75cm x 3cm),
2014

Standing wool using glue with 100% upcycled Australian wool blankets left as is or overdyed with food coloring.

LATA PHOTOGRAPHY

So What,
$51^1/_2$" x 48" x $1^1/_4$"
(131 cm x 122 cm x 3 cm),
2014

Standing wool using glue with 100% upcycled Australian wool blankets left as is or overdyed with food coloring.

LATA PHOTOGRAPHY

The Reef,
33¹/₂″ x 33¹/₂″ x 1¹/₄″
(85 cm x 85 cm x 3 cm),
2015

Standing wool using glue with
100% upcycled Australian wool
blankets left as is or overdyed
with food coloring.

LATA PHOTOGRAPHY

Aurora,
42¹/₂″ x 36¹/₄″ x 1¹/₄″
(108 cm x 92 cm x 3 cm),
2015

Standing wool using glue with
100% upcycled Australian wool
blankets left as is or overdyed
with food coloring.

LATA PHOTOGRAPHY

Cosmic Peacock,
37³/₄" x 37³/₄" x 1¹/₄"
(96 cm x 96 cm x 3 cm),
2015

Standing wool using glue with
100% upcycled Australian wool
blankets, left as is or overdyed
with food coloring, and imbedded
LED fairy lights.

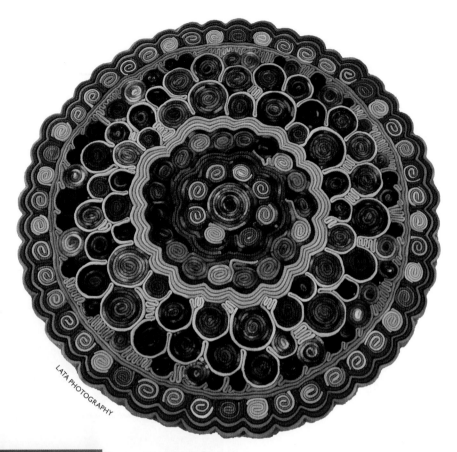

LATA PHOTOGRAPHY

Le Tourbillon Derrière,
40¹/₂" x 24¹/₂" (103 cm x 62 cm),
2015

Standing wool using glue with 100% upcycled
Australian wool blankets left as is or overdyed with
food coloring.

LATA PHOTOGRAPHY

Kris Miller

Howell, Michigan, U.S.; www.spruceridgestudios.com

Kris has been rug hooking since 1998 and is primarily self-taught. She learned the coiling technique, though she refers to it as quilling, from Ali Strebel. Kris has been designing hooking patterns since 2000 and teaches wide cut and primitive hooking in the United States and England. She wrote *Introduction to Rug Hooking*, published by Stackpole Books in February 2015.

Paisleys, woven coverlets, and any type of textile with an intricate design fascinate her. She also knits and spins; she lives on a small farm in Michigan with sheep, angora goats, and two alpacas.

Detail of **Fancy Barn Symbol,**
18.5" (47 cm) round,
2011

Hooking with coiled bird wing in wool on linen. Pennsylvania barn symbols were the inspiration for this piece; the full image can be seen on her website.

Sheepish Pillow,
13¹/₂" x 17" x 4"
(34.3 cm x 43.2 cm x 10.2 cm),
2009

Beaded hooking around the edge with coiled embellishments, in wool on linen.

Emma, Kris's Wensleydale sheep, was her inspiration for this pillow.

Laurie Wiles

Edmonton, Alberta, Canada

Laurie has been working with fibers since 1996. She learned rug hooking and other techniques with the Edmonton Rug Hooking Guild and Gail Becker.

Galaxies,
19" x 11" (48.3 cm x 27.9 cm),
2012

Traditional hooking and coiling with wool, beads, and charms.

"When I think about the night sky I think about the space above us. I wanted to experiment with color and texture to form my own vision of the night sky. I tried to re-create galaxies spinning and forming the heavens. I want to share my wonder of the vastness of space with others through my art."

Laurie used wool strips to make swirls and represented the planets forming by using quillies within the universe. The piece was completed with three planets moving within their own atmospheres.

LAURIE WILES

Leisa Rich

Denton, Texas and Atlanta, Georgia, U.S.; www.monaleisa.com

Leisa has been working in fiber arts and mixed media since 1975. She has an MFA and undergraduate degrees in fine art and art education. She uses old materials in new ways and new materials in unexpected ways. She had never seen this technique at the time she started doing it; it is now a common construction method used by many artists working with fibers.

in(CONSEQUENTIAL), *240" x 60" x 12" (610 cm x 152.5 cm x 30.5 cm), variable, 2007*

Wool and plastic drinking straws dyed, rolled, sliced, glued, stitched, and assembled.

"Little things kicked aside and considered unimportant—a tiny chip of sparkly stone encountered during a walk, a bit of textured metal clinging to a storm drain in summer rain, or a broken piece of sun-bleached sunglasses snagged in a tangled cluster of moss—can become consequential and worth notice when gathered together.

"In creating pieces that reference some sort of 'nature' formed from human manufactured elements, I am tempting viewers to notice: titillating with texture, wooing them with organic form, delighting them with color, and inviting them to notice a new reality I birthed that is part of a Utopian environment that exists in my mind.

"In the creation of this installation, a collection of parts that can be reformed in myriad configurations and variations, I used hundreds of yards of wool felt and hundreds of plastic drinking straws, and hundreds of glue sticks and worked on it over hundreds of

hours. Initially, I saw this piece exist on a much, much grander scale; limitations of money, time, and space, and being the single person on the task, meant I had to scale the work back. *(in)CONSEQUENTIAL* stands on its own, but was meant to be part of a larger place to wonder."

in(CONSEQUENTIAL)
In progress

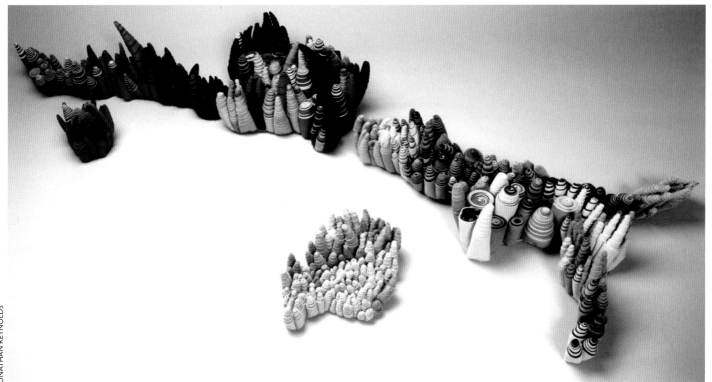

Liquid Force, *60" x 48" x 4" (152.5 cm x 122 cm x 10.2 cm), variable, 2006*

Wool dyed, rolled, sliced, glued, stitched, and assembled.

"I exponentially magnify many organic structures, letting them multiply in my studio Petri dish. Like a single plant cell or disease that replicates over and over again over time, becoming a unique organism that changes and takes new form, my pieces also morph. I am often stepping over them in my studio as they evolve, realizing that the initial artistic power I had to control them into a specific shape is now gone. I let them take over. I have a unique 'natural' world of my making in which to superficially exist. *Liquid Force,* formed by dyeing and rolling dozens of lengths of wool felt, references ripples of water and the ever-changing variations of blue, green, and gray of the lakes of my youth. It took about 24 hours to construct."

Detail of **Liquid Force**

JONATHAN REYNOLDS

Rhodochrosite, *28" x 120" x 10" (71 cm x 305 cm x 25.4 cm), variable, 2007*

Wool dyed, rolled, sliced, glued, stitched, and assembled.

"I grew up in Canada surrounded by lovely, wide-open spaces, fabulous lakes, and awe-inspiring mountains and a very low human population. I felt, and continue to feel, most at peace in the natural world. I had a childhood filled with the delights of nature: ice skating outdoors on natural creeks, glistening icicles that magically transformed my backyard into a glittering diamond mine, days spent happily alone for hours sifting among the sand on the beach of Lake Huron in quest of a perfect fossil. I took walks through forest that never seemed to end without seeing another soul, camped out under stars I could actually see in an unpolluted sky, and exalted in moments spent completely still, watching caterpillars miraculously transform into butterflies. I possessed an existence of wonderment and pure, unadulterated joy, given me by the simple bits in nature. Each day I try to transform ordinary, everyday things I see, using readily available materials, into extraordinary sculptural forms in order to give greater significance to them. The pieces I create are not meant to 'reproduce' bits of the world as one might see in realism—in this case the mineral rhodochrosite—but merely represent an 'aura' I get from them. I used several yards of wool felt and dyes, and rolled tight spirals into clusters in the creation of this piece. It took about 36 hours to construct."

JONATHAN REYNOLDS

Detail of **Rhodochrosite**

Liz Alpert Fay

Sandy Hook, Connecticut, U.S.; www.lizalpertfay.com
   Liz has been interested in fibers since childhood. In 1981 she earned a degree in textile design from the Program in Artisanry at Boston University, and later learned the beaded rug technique from a pamphlet on rug techniques.

Tree Skirt #2-Untitled,
13¹/₂" x 21¹/₂" x 17"
(34.3 cm x 54.6 cm x 43.2 cm),
2007

Beaded rug technique and spool knitting with found wood, wool, thread, and cotton yarn.
   This piece is part of Liz's series celebrating various types of found wood.

BRAD STANTON

Detail of **Tree Skirt #2-Untitled**

Mary DeLano

Norway, Maine, U.S.

Mary works primarily with wool fabric, creating sewn and knitted rugs using historical techniques and wool appliqué pieces with lots of embellishments. She typically does not sew her rugs onto a backing so that they are two-sided. She learned shirring in 2010 from rug historian and teacher Rose Ann Hunter.

Mary "loves color and texture and enjoys teaching students new techniques that allow them to create their own unique pieces."

Rainbow Runner,
134" x 30" (340.4 cm x 76.2 cm),
2013

Standing wool, beading, center shirring, and faux shirring using new and recycled wool and cotton crochet thread.

After making a small coaster, Mary started working on this piece; it took her over two years to finish, and yes, they do walk on it but not while wearing shoes. Mary found wool in thrift shops and purchased more from braiders and rug hookers via Craig's List. She increased her color palette by dyeing wool in a Crock-Pot. New wool was purchased and dyed for hard-to-find colors, such as orange and yellow.

She sewed individual flowers in one color, and then joined them into larger pieces, filling in gaps with "plugs." Working with larger pieces, she used a curved needle so the pieces would remain flat. She made six separate pieces before joining them. The finished piece was bound with black strips sewn through the middle, and each row was cut narrower than the previous row so that the edge would taper to reduce the tripping hazard.

MARY DELANO

ANNE STUER

LINDA NOONAN

Detail of **Rainbow Runner**

Brown Trivet
9" (22.9 cm) diameter,
2012

Standing wool, beading, and faux shirring using recycled wool and cotton crochet thread.

Since Mary is normally a lover of bright colors, this was a challenge to work in a muted palette. She made it while she was working on *Rainbow Runner* to have completion on a project as the runner took so long to make.

Purple Circle,
18" (45.7 cm) diameter, ³/₄"
(1.9 cm) high,
2014

Caterpillar (chenille) shirring with recycled wool and cotton crochet thread.

Braided rugs that have three separate circles joined by several rows of braiding were Mary's inspiration for this piece. She has also made circles in blue and green and has plans to join them all together.

Caterpillar shirring starts as regular center shirring. The wool is shirred down the center of the strip, and then the wool is twisted around the thread to make the caterpillar. The caterpillar is coiled and sewn to itself, much as with standing wool. Mary usually sews back through two existing rows as she adds each new row to give the rug more

support. "It can be a bit tricky to keep all of the thread hidden. It tends to poke through the surface more often than with standing wool."

Rebecca Townsend

Forest City, Pennsylvania, U.S.; www.milkweedandpoppyseed.com

Rebecca started working with standing wool around 2010, using old wool clothes from relatives, with a desire to make a rug for her home. She is strongly committed to sustainability, using only reclaimed wool.

"I am self-taught through trial and error after seeing a few photos online. I learned to sew, both by hand and machine at an early age, so this was just one more extension of those skills." She avoids making large pieces; though she loves the process and results, "it takes more time than one might realize."

Harvest Table Centerpiece, *38" x 19" x ³/₄"*
(96.5 cm x 48.3 cm x 1.9 cm), February 2015

Coiling and standing wool with reclaimed lamb's wool and merino wool sweaters.

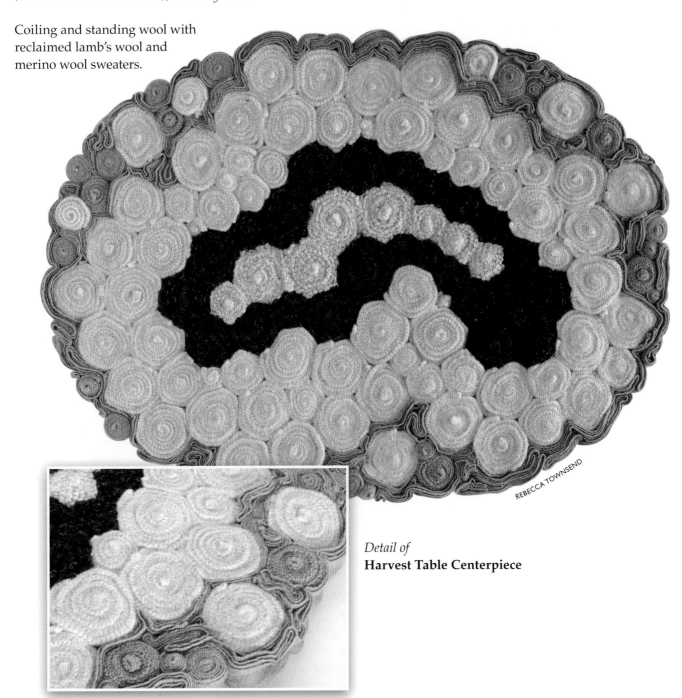

REBECCA TOWNSEND

Detail of
Harvest Table Centerpiece

REBECCA TOWNSEND

Trees, *3–5" x 3" x ³/₄" (7.6–12.7 cm x 1.9 cm), 2014*

Coiling and standing wool with various reclaimed wool and cashmere sweaters and skirts.

Charm,
2–3" x 2–3" x ³/₄"
(5.1–7.6 cm x 5.1–7.6 cm x 1.9 cm),
2014

Coiling and standing wool with various reclaimed wool and cashmere sweaters and skirts.

After washing the clothing, Rebecca cut strips ³/₄" (1.9 cm) wide with a rotary cutter and mat, cutting knits vertically and wovens on the bias. Strips are hand-rolled into coils and hand-sewn securely with a curved needle. She prefers the coils or strips to be tightly sewn when assembled, which is a very time-consuming process.

REBECCA TOWNSEND

Rita Vail

Marion, Montana, U.S.

  Rita started rug hooking in 2000 and quilling in 2012 and says she has been taught by "amazing teachers."

Petroglyph Hunt, *21" x 17" (53.3 cm x 43.2 cm), April 2015*

Quilling and traditional rug hooking with hand-dyed Dorr wool and hand-dyed knitting worsted yarn.
  Rita created this piece in Green Valley, Arizona, but it was inspired by photos taken in Renegade Canyon, California.

Rose Ann Hunter

Newburyport, Massachusetts, U.S.; www.roseannhunter.com; Rose Ann Hunter on Facebook

Rose Ann has been working with fiber and teaching fiber arts since 1975. She has been using shirring and standing wool techniques since 2005.

While working at various museums, Rose Ann was intrigued by objects made with wool scraps. Her research on these objects in museum storage and in old journals inspired her to design pieces using the early techniques with a contemporary feel.

TRACY JAMAR

Pincushions,
3–4" x 4–5"
(7.6–10.2 cm x 10.2–12.7 cm),
various widths $^1/_4$–$1^3/_4$" *(.6–3.2 cm),*
2014

Stacked standing wool, center shirring, caterpillar shirring, or faux shirring with wool.

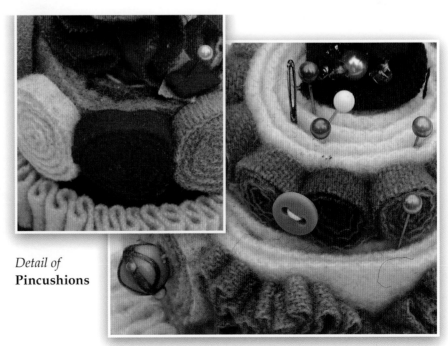

Detail of
Pincushions

Sheep Whimsies, *4"–6" x 3^1/$_2$"–7^1/$_2$" (10.2–15.2 cm x 8.9–19.1 cm),*
various widths ^{3}/$_8$"–^{5}/$_8$" (1–1.6 cm), 2014

Standing wool, center shirring, caterpillar shirring, or faux shirring with wool.

Quillie Bracelets,
8^1/$_2$"–10" (21.6–25.4 cm) x ^{1}/$_4$" (.6 cm),
2014

Beading and button shirring with
patch shirring embellishments
with wool.

Sarah McNamara

Greenport, New York, U.S.; https://www.etsy.com/shop/thepaisleystudio; http://paisleystudio.blogspot.com
  Sarah has been creating works with rug hooking since 1990. She learned the standing wool technique in 2005 at a class on historical rugs taught by Nola Heidbreder and Linda Pietz at Hooked in the Mountains, Vermont.

Blue and Green Scrumble,
4¹/₂″ x 4³/₄″ (11.4 cm x 11.1 cm),
2000

Standing wool technique with wool.
  This piece was inspired by the knit and crochet scrumbles of Prudence Mapstone.

Circular Santa,
12″ (30.5 cm) diameter,
December 2014

Rug hooking and standing wool with wool on linen.
  Circular Santa is available as a pattern from Sarah's website.

TRACY JAMAR

TRACY JAMAR

Leaping Rabbit,
8³/4" x 4¹/4", hanger 8¹/2"
(22.2 cm x 10.8 cm, hanger 21.6 cm),
March 2014

Rug hooking and standing wool
with wool on linen.

Quilly Heart,
8¹/2" x 9", hanger 7"
(21.6 cm x 22.9 cm, hanger 17.8 cm),
March 2015

Rug hooking, standing wool, and fabric
twisted with wool on linen.

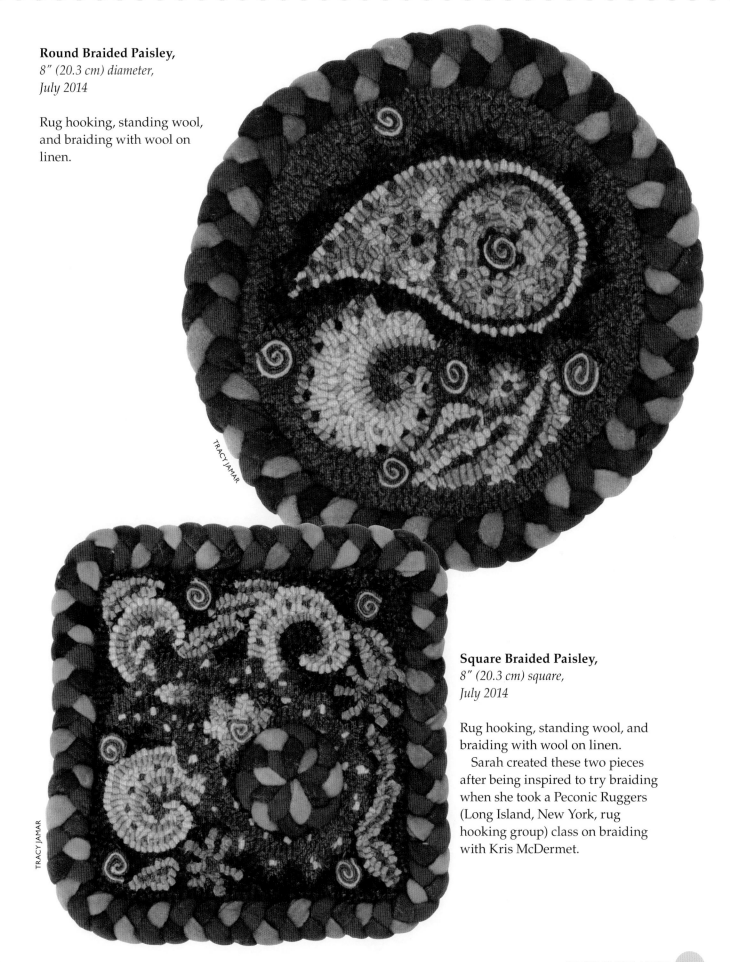

Round Braided Paisley,
8" (20.3 cm) diameter,
July 2014

Rug hooking, standing wool,
and braiding with wool on
linen.

TRACY JAMAR

Square Braided Paisley,
8" (20.3 cm) square,
July 2014

Rug hooking, standing wool, and
braiding with wool on linen.
  Sarah created these two pieces
after being inspired to try braiding
when she took a Peconic Ruggers
(Long Island, New York, rug
hooking group) class on braiding
with Kris McDermet.

TRACY JAMAR

TRACY JAMAR

Snowman and Snowballs,
6¹/₂" x 10" (17.1 cm x 25.4 cm),
December 2014

Rug hooking and standing
wool with wool on linen.

Tide Pool,
8¹/₂" (21.6 cm) square,
2000

Rug hooking and standing
wool with wool on linen.

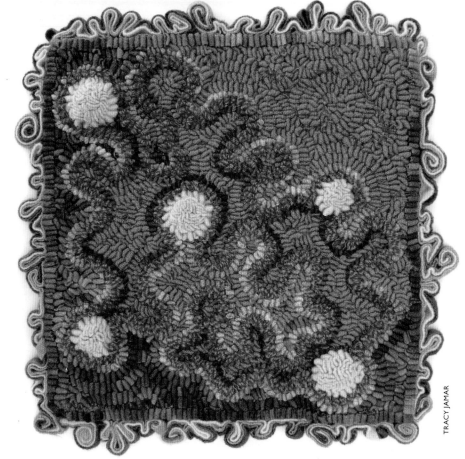

TRACY JAMAR

Susan Feller

Augusta, West Virginia, U.S.; www.RuckmanMillFarm.com; www.ArtWools.com/year-study

Susan's involvement with fiber techniques has evolved since childhood. She used paper quilling and gold leaf back in 1990 for custom picture framing, but was influenced to develop the technique with fabric after seeing the American Sewn Rug exhibit at Sauder Village in 2013.

These pieces were selected from Susan's project *The Year Study*, where she created a 5" x 5" (12.7 cm x 12.7 cm) piece each day for 365 days, an exploration in discipline, direction, and design.

"Looking around for an academic program to focus learning skills, I decided an independent study conducted with myself as student and advisor would fulfill the quest." Her goal was to "explore techniques, materials, and composition on a daily basis for one year. Evaluate the work with consideration of direction to concentrate developing body of work. Exhibit the collection. Document the process and lessons. Complete the squares for sale."

The other squares may be seen on her website listed above.

Navels,
5" x 5" (12.7 cm x 12.7 cm),
2014

Appliqué, prodding, quilling, trapunto, painting, and hooking with wool fabric and paint on linen.

Oranges outside her guest room window in New Mexico in January were the inspiration for *Navels*. She wanted to "explore as many different techniques as possible with the circle shape."

Sunflower,
5" x 5" (12.7 cm x 12.7 cm),
2014

Hooking and standing wool with wool fabric on linen.
The sunflower is Susan's favorite flower.
"In *The Year Study* several techniques portray flowers. Standing wool is bold and allowed continuous lines of color after the common circle shape."

Turmoil,
5" x 5" (12.7 cm x 12.7 cm),
2014

Standing wool with wool fabric
on linen.
   "A sketch of lines circling
out into chaos guided the
construction. In response to the
date 9.11 and continued strife in
the world. Colors are red, white,
blue = USA and many other
countries' flags, also symbolizes
freedom yet conflict in 2014."

SUSAN FELLER

Hayrolls,
5" x 5" (12.7 cm x 12.7 cm),
2013

Quilling, appliqué, and hooking
with wool fabric on linen.
   Susan used a #6 cut for both
hooking and quilling, which gave
the effect of rolled hay.

SUSAN FELLER

Marilyn Bottjer

Eastchester, New York, U.S.

Marilyn has been working with fibers since the early 1960s, and in 1966 she found a hooking class and fell in love with the technique. She is an innovator in her rug hooking with techniques, styles, and materials, however only used proddy and coiling in the last few years.

She has been teaching since 1970 in various venues including the American Folk Art Museum in New York City. Her work has been exhibited nationally and internationally, and Linda Rae Coughlin profiled her in *Rug Hooking* magazine's Readers' Gallery in the September/October 2015 issue.

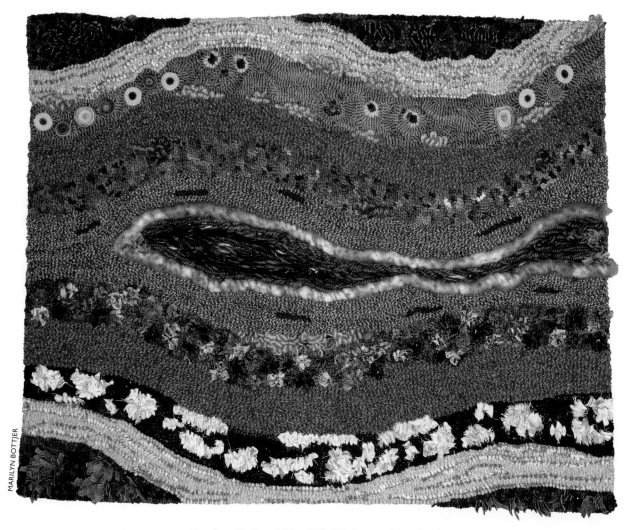

Garden Paths, *22" x 26" (55.8 cm x 66 cm), 2015*

Traditional hooking, proddy, and coiling using hand-dyed wool fabric and yarns, silk, and cotton on linen foundation.

Marilyn's inspiration was found in the book *Japanese Stripes and Splashes* by Furuya Setsuzan, Dover Pictorial Archive Series, 2011. This is a collection of "authentic Japanese woodblock designs reproduced from early twentieth century patterns designed for use on fabrics."

Susie Brandt

Baltimore, Maryland, U.S.
   Susie invented the technique she uses and has been working with traditional and innovated techniques since 1987.

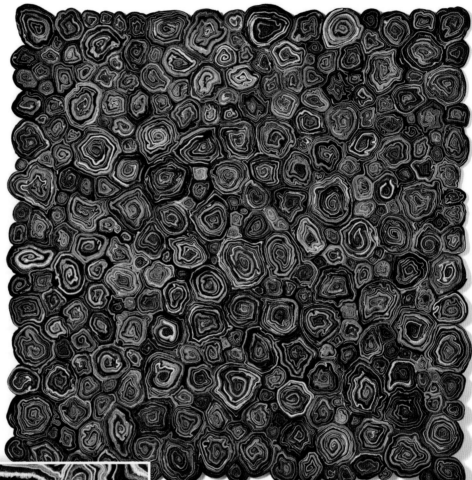

DAN MEYERS

Slice,
73" x 73" x 1" (185.4 cm x 185.4 cm x 2.54 cm),
2011

Hand-stitched wool fabric.
   Slice is one of two pieces commissioned from Susie; one is hanging at the University of Michigan C.S. Mott Children's Hospital and the other at Von Voigtlander Women's Hospital in Ann Arbor, Michigan.

Detail of **Slice**

Tracy Jamar

New York, New York, U.S.; www.tracyjamar.com; Tracy Jamar FiberWorks on Facebook

"It is sometimes hard to pinpoint the inspiration for any one piece. Some ferment in my mind for years and others are upon me in a flash, but it is usually a combination of things: a color, fabrics, a photo, a statement to be made, textures, techniques to try, works by others, and antique pieces (fiber and not), that urges me to create something.

"I have always worked with my hands and appreciated the handwork of others in a wide variety of arts, trades, and crafts. As a child I knitted, in high school I sewed clothing. In the 1970s I participated in craft fairs, selling beaded and macramé items. When I became involved in the antiques business, antique textiles became my primary interest. I began antique restoration work on quilts for America Hurrah Gallery when I moved to NYC from Minnesota in 1979, which led to working on hooked rugs. I learned hooking mostly from the pieces I worked on and from the illustrations of techniques in *American Hooked and Sewn Rugs: Folk Art Underfoot* by Joel and Kate Kopp.

"I did not start making my own hooked pieces until 1994 when I made a memorial to a beloved horse, Arrow, using old t-shirts. Though I still enjoy the other fiber pursuits, it has been hooking and related rug techniques that have been my creative mainstay.

"After nearly 30 years in antique textile restoration, I went back to college to finish a degree long delayed. In 2009 I graduated from Goddard College, in Vermont, where I studied an individualized and independent program on American history through women's handmade textiles. That experience affirmed my desire to retire from restoration and create my own works using a combination of techniques with a wide variety of materials."

Tossed, Circumference 69" (175.25 cm) x height 8" (20.3 cm), 2016.

Coiling and gluing with wool (1,475 strips)
to found stainless steel mixing bowl.

Well Rounded,
4" x 5¹/₄" x 6⁷/₈"
(10.2 cm x 13.25 cm x 17.1 cm),
2015

Coiled wool Melton glued to painted and paper-covered wood cigar box.

"This was made for a fund-raising auction where artists were invited to decorate and donate a box."

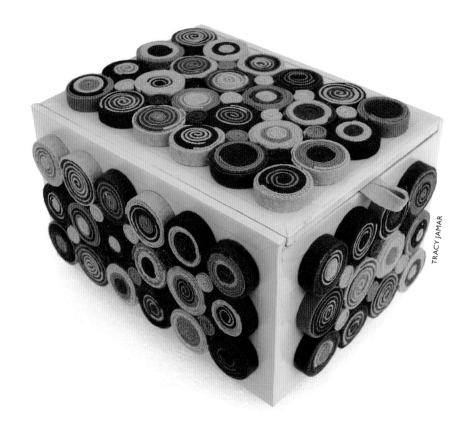

TRACY JAMAR

Beach Drift,
9" x 9" x 3"
(22.9 cm x 22.9 cm x 7.6 cm),
2011

Folded fabric squares, bias shirring, and embroidery with overdyed wool, cotton, and silk fabrics and specialty yarn on linen mounted in painted wood box.

TRACY JAMAR

Checked Out,
32" x 16" (81.3 cm x 40.6 cm),
2011

Hand- and machine-sewn shredded bank checks and hand hooked shredded dollar bills on linen mounted on cotton flannel.

"In preparation for moving, I shredded many old checks—running my fingers through them, I loved how they felt and decided I could not toss them. It was also when the recession was ever present and these checks were a history of my financial situation for several years. I consider this a contemporary variation or an expanded interpretation of shirring."

Detail of **Checked Out**

TRACY JAMAR

Cut Back,
18¹/₄" x 24¹/₄"
(46.4 cm x 61.6 cm),
2014

Hand-sewn and hooked
wool from damaged woven
rag rug, wool, and yarn on
monk's cloth.

   "A leaky plant pot damaged
a rag runner; I cut the rug
down, but could not bear to
throw the rag strips away. The
sun-faded lines on the strips
have an interesting texture.
Might this be considered 'flat'
standing wool?"

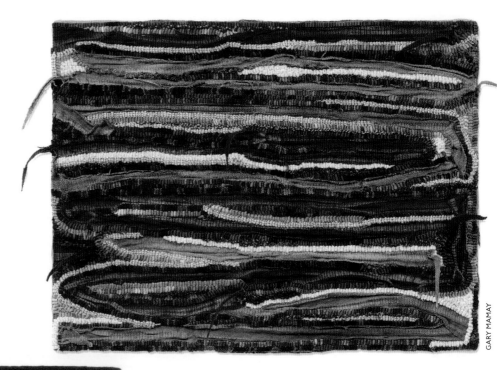

GARY MAMAY

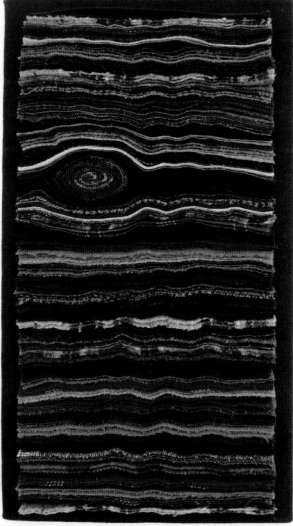

TRACY JAMAR

Fiber Eddy,
21" x 12" (53.3 cm x 30.9 cm),
2015

Hand- and machine-sewing with wool and wool
blends on cotton flannel.

   "I was given a lot of wool fabrics, not all appropriate
for hooking. I wanted to see how they looked in a very
simple pattern."

Fossil,
12" x 12" (30.5 cm x 30.5 cm),
2013

Hooking, bias and chenille shirring with repurposed denim and printed cotton on monk's cloth.

TRACY JAMAR

Detail of
Fossil

Furrows,
23" x 34" (58.4 cm x 86.4 cm),
2014

Appliqué, hooking, bias and chenille shirring with vintage wool challis quilt squares and wool on monk's cloth.
   "I have many antique fabrics and used unassembled strip squares as the center of this piece."

TRACY JAMAR

Harvest,
24" x 27"
(61 cm x 68.6 cm),
2013

Hooking, bias and chenille shirring with wool and wool blends on monk's cloth.

"This was a study in texture and light and dark. Many feel that the light and dark do not work well together—that tension is what I like the most about this piece."

GARY MAMAY

Hedgerows,
29³/4" x 31¹/2" (75.6 cm x 80 cm),
2011

Hooking, bias shirring, coiling, fringing and appliqué with wool, cotton, and synthetic fibers on linen.

"I was given some lovely expensive linen, and rather than cover it up with hooking, I left some of it exposed."

GARY MAMAY

Merge,
17" x 17" (43.2 cm x 43.2 cm),
2013

Coiling, machine- and hand-sewing with wool swatches and strips on cotton duck.

   "This was to use up many wool swatches and leftover wool strips."

TRACY JAMAR

Ripples, *24" x 24",*
made up of four 12" x 12" sections (61 cm x 61 cm, four 30.5 cm x 30.5 cm sections),
2014

Hooking and bias shirring with wool, cotton, silk, and mixed fibers on monk's cloth.

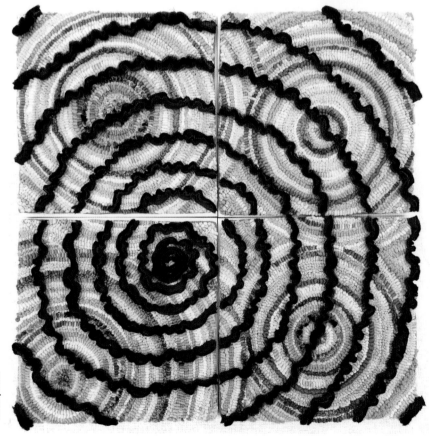

TRACY JAMAR

Tide Pools,
9" x 9" x 3"
(22.9 cm x 22.9 cm x 7.6 cm),
2011

Bias shirring, embroidery, coiling, and beading with overdyed wool, vintage wool shawl, cotton thread, and glass beads on linen mounted in painted wood box.

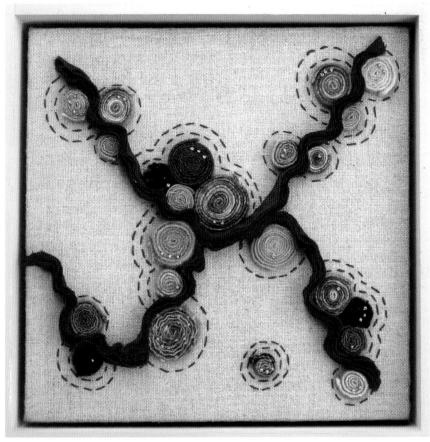

TRACY JAMAR

Wandering,
9" x 9" x 3"
(22.9 cm x 22.9 cm x 7.6 cm),
2011

Bias shirring, coiling, hooking, and beading with wool, antique paisley shawl, yarns, and glass beads on linen mounted in painted wood box.

TRACY JAMAR

The following rug sample photos were used in the book *American Sewn Rugs: Their History with Exceptional Examples* to illustrate the different techniques.

GARY MAMAY

GARY MAMAY

Chenille Shirred, *11" x 11"*
(27.9 cm x 27.9 cm), 2011
Chenille shirring with wool, antique paisley shawl, and silk on cotton twill.

Bias Shirred, *11" x 11"*
(27.9 cm x 27.9 cm), 2010
Bias shirring with wool, antique paisley shawl, and silk on cotton twill.

Pleated/Bundled, *11" x 11"*
(27.9 cm x 27.9 cm), 2010
Pleating and bundled shirring with wool yarn and fabric on cotton twill.

Contemporary, *11" x 11"*
(27.9 cm x 27.9 cm), 2014
Hooking, shirring, fringing, appliqué, beading, and coiling with wool, silk, and glass beads on monk's cloth.

This piece was not used in *American Sewn Rugs*, but was one of two added to illustrate more contemporary fabric techniques.

Rug Samples, *Each is 11" x 11" (27.9 cm x 27.9 cm)*

With the nine pieces using the same design and coloring, it is easy to compare the details of the different techniques—appliqué, yarn sewing, tambour, chenille shirring, bias shirring, pleating/bundling, hooking, needle punching, and contemporary—with various fabrics and yarns.

Seven of these samples were made for inclusion in *American Sewn Rugs: Their History with Exceptional Examples*; tambour and contemporary were completed later. As needle punch is worked from the back, the design has been reversed.

Conclusion

I hope you find pleasure, inspiration, and fulfillment in what you have seen here. May you be entranced and enticed to try your own hand in using these techniques. They are not difficult, and can be made with just about any material, and the more you do, the more variety you will discover to do.

Acknowledgments

How far back do you go to acknowledge and thank those for the support and encouragement you have received in recognition of where you are today? It is a long chain of connections and associations that brings one to her current place.

To parents who were doers and makers in their own right as models. To friends along the way with mutual appreciation and encouragement. To a broken relationship that propelled me to NYC, where Kate and Joel Kopp offered me a job at America Hurrah Gallery. It was there I was immersed in exposure to and restoration of the finest in antique American textiles. To Jan Whitlock, not only for trusting me with her exceptional textile projects and inviting me to take part in her book idea, which inspired this book, but to a friendship as well. To Debra Smith, editor of *Rug Hooking Magazine*, for the offer of writing this book, which has expanded my creative world in many wonderful ways. To the community of fiber folks who inspire, share, and challenge each other to experiment and explore new things. To my husband, Monty Silver, for his appreciation and encouragement in my fiber pursuits and for his patience and well-tested tolerance in allowing me to spread my projects (almost) everywhere.

Thank you all!

Resources

Check the artists' pages in the Gallery section of this book for their websites. Many artists, publications, and organizations also have Facebook pages.

PUBLICATIONS

Fiber Art Now magazine—http://fiberartnow.net

Rug Hooking Magazine—http://www.rughooking magazine.com

BOOKS

Gray, Diana Blake. A variety of rug making books and pamphlets are available at www.rugmakers homestead.com.

Kopp, Joel, and Kate Kopp, *American Hooked and Sewn Rugs: Folk Art Under Foot*. New York: E. P. Dutton & Co. Inc., 1975.

Stackpole Books—http://www.stackpolebooks.com

Whitlock, Jan, with Tracy Jamar, *American Sewn Rugs: Their History with Exceptional Examples*. Privately printed, 2012.

Wolff, Colette, *The Art of Manipulating Fabric*. Iola, WI: Krause Publications, 1996.

ORGANIZATIONS

Association of Traditional Hooking Artists (ATHA)—www.atharugs.com

The International Guild of Handhooking Rugmakers (TIGHR)—www.tighr.net

Green Mountain Rug Hooking Guild—www.gmrhg .org

Australian Rugmakers Guild—http://www.rug hookingaustralia.com.au

Sauder Village Rug Hooking Week (held every August)—http://www.saudervillage.org/ Creativity/rughooking.asp

FACEBOOK PAGES

Critical Craft Forum

Fiber Artist Guild

Fiber Arts/Mixed Media Art

Hooked Rugs and Proddy Mats

Making Rugs—Hooked, Prodded . . .

Paper Threads, Yarns, and Textiles

Quillie Rugs

Rag Ruggers

Rug Hooking-Camps, Shows, Workshops, and Classes

Standing Wool Rugmaking

Tracy Jamar FiberWorks

Textile Arts

Wool 'n Folk

ADDITIONAL ARTISTS' WEBSITES

Cilla Cameron—http://www.ragrugsuk.co.uk

Gail Dufresne—http://www.goathilldesigns.com

Nola Heidbreder—www.nolahooks.com

Wanda Kerr—http://www.wandaworks.ca

Prudence Mapstone—www.knotjustknitting.com

Kris McDermet—www.krismcdermet.com

VIDEOS OF INTEREST

"DIY Rug Made of Felt Scraps"—http://www.shelter ness.com/diy-rug-made-of-felt-scraps/

"The Making of Accidental Carpet"—https://www .youtube.com/watch?v=J8YSaAF0sxY